Easy Paper-Pieced Keepsake Quilts

72 Quilt Blocks for Foundation Piecing

CAROL DOAK

Credits

Editor-in-Chief ....Barbara Weiland
Technical Editor...Janet White
Managing Editor ....Greg Sharp
Copy Editor...Tina Cook
Proofreader ....Leslie Phillips
Design Director ....Judy Petry
Text and Cover Designer ....Cheryl Stevenson
Design Assistant ....Claudia L'Heureux
Illustrators ....Carolyn Kraft
Laurel Strand
Illustration Assistant ....Lisa McKenney
Photographer ....Brent Kane

Easy Paper-Pieced Keepsake Quilts
© 1995 by Carol Doak
That Patchwork Place, Inc., PO Box 118, Bothell, WA
98041-0118 USA

Printed in Hong Kong
00 99 98 97 96   6 5 4

Library of Congress Cataloging-in-Publication Data
Doak, Carol.
    Paper-Pieced Keepsake Quilts / Carol Doak.
       p. cm.
    ISBN 1-56477-109-1
    1. Patchwork—Patterns. 2. Machine Quilting.
    3. Patchwork quilts. I. Title.
TT835.D627   1995
746.46—dc20   95–6594
                       CIP

Dedication

To Mo Clegg, Peggy Forand, Ginny Guaraldi, Pam Ludwig, Beth Meek, Terry Maddox, and Mary Kay Sieve for making every Wednesday so special.

Acknowledgments

My heartfelt thanks and appreciation go to:

Sherry Reis, Pam Ludwig, Peggy Forand, Beth Meek, Ginny Guaraldi, Moira Clegg, Mary Kay Sieve, Terry Maddox, Helen Weinman, and Marion Shelton for shar-ing their wonderful paper-pieced keepsake quilts, and for their treasured friendship and support.

Penny McMorris, for a delightful friendship that blossomed from our mutual appreciation for paper-pieced patterns drawn on the computer.

Al and Nancy Pater at Minuteman Press, for their friendly smiles and extra courtesies each time I came by to make copies.

The many workshop participants, for their infec-tious enthusiasm for machine paper piecing and their encouragement to push the limits. They have made teaching this technique a pure joy.

Barbara Weiland, Ursula Reikes, Janet White, Marion Shelton, and the entire staff at That Patchwork Place for their friendship, expertise, and support.

Contents

Preface

My first book about foundation piecing, *Easy Machine Paper Piecing,* was the product of my deep appreciation for the paper-piecing method. I appreciated the immediate gratification of going to the sewing machine with paper pattern and fabric in hand to begin piecing my blocks. I appreciated the quilts that resulted from the variety of block designs. In this book, a new collection of designs offers the same accuracy and immediate gratification, with yet another avenue for appreciation.

As I worked with the designs for this book, a theme began to emerge. Messages of love and peace appeared in many forms. The Letter blocks brought forth a "Welcome" quilt and the opportunity to personalize quilts. The Flower, Basket, and Heart blocks inspired a special wedding quilt and quilts that celebrate the seasons. One block design often led to another as I worked to create keepsake quilts. These designs offer many opportunities to make quick and easy keepsake quilts for gift giving and tributes to life's many celebrations.

Introduction

The concept of paper piecing is a simple one. A design with a straight-seam sequence is drawn on paper. Over-size fabric pieces are placed in sequence on the un-marked side of the paper, and the lines are sewn from the marked side of the paper. After each seam is sewn, the seam allowance is trimmed, and the piece is folded open. Once the quilt top is complete, the paper is torn away from the stitching. There is no template making or fabric marking, and no high degree of skill is needed to piece blocks accurately.

Easy Paper-Pieced Keepsake Quilts is modeled after *Easy Machine Paper Piecing.* You can use the two books together or separately. The blocks in both books are presented in the same format and in the same size, so you can easily combine these blocks with the sixty-five designs in *Easy Machine Paper Piecing.*

The mechanics of paper piecing are the same in both books; however, in this book I have introduced a few two-section blocks in the "Quilt Blocks" section. Two sections of a block are pieced as separate units and then joined. How to create the reverse of an asymmetrical block is introduced in the "Working with Block Designs" section. These new designs are grouped in the following categories: Geometrics, Flowers, Hearts and Baskets, Trees, Pictures, Letters, and Christmas designs.

The letters of the alphabet offer many opportunities to personalize your quilts and include messages. You will find many suggestions in the Block and Quilt Design Possibilities section. The keepsake theme also inspires many opportunities to create small patchwork gifts, and I have provided several ideas.

The quilts in the Gallery of Quilts represent just a fraction of the arrangements possible for this latest group of paper-pieced designs. Quilts are shown in several different sizes and styles and celebrate the seasons, holidays, love, peace, a new baby, patriotism, and friendship. What better reason to make a quilt than as a remembrance of a special event?

I hope you have a wonderful time and feel a sense of gratification as you create your keepsake quilts.

Working with Block Designs

The 4" block designs are full size and ready to use. The numbers on the block designs indicate the piecing sequence. The seam between piece #1 and piece #2 is sewn first, and the remaining seams follow in sequence. Some of the block designs require a unit with one or two prepieced seams. Pieced units are identified on the block pattern with a "//" through the seam and are explained in greater detail on pages 12–13. A few of the blocks are two-section blocks and are pieced as separate units that are joined to form the block. This procedure is described on page 12.

Reproducing Block Designs

Tracing

Place a piece of tracing paper on top of the 4" block design and secure it with masking tape to keep the paper from shifting while drawing. Using a mechanical pencil and ruler, trace the lines, markings, and numbers. Make a separate tracing for each block.

Although tracing the blocks by hand takes more time than using the photocopy machine, it does offer advantages. The lines are easier to see during the design and sewing process, and the paper is easier to remove.

Photocopying

You can use a photocopy machine to reproduce the blocks; however, photocopy machines do produce copies with variances. Photocopying a 4" original block can produce a block that is just a "hair" larger (less than 1%). The blocks can be ever so slightly off square. A perfect square has identical diagonal measurements from corner to corner. A photocopy can have a variance of approximately ⅟₁₆". This variance is so slight and occurs over such a great distance that normally you cannot see it. However, because it will compound the variance, it is not advisable to make a copy from a copy. The designs for each project should all be copied from the original block, on the same machine. Different photocopy ma-

chines may produce copies with a different variance. Always be sure that the copied blocks are the correct size for the intended project. Use a rotary cutter and acrylic square ruler to trim photocopies ½" from the outside finished block lines on all sides.

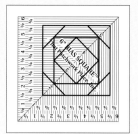

Enlarging and Reducing Block Designs

The lure of changing the size of the original block led me to investigate the reducing and enlarging options on the photocopy machine. After much experimentation, I concluded that all enlargements and reductions for a chosen design should be made from the original patterns and on the same photocopy machine. You can reduce copies to 64% and enlarge them to 156%. The same variance applies to blocks that you enlarge or reduce. A 3" block is 75% of the original, a 5" block is 125% of the original, and a 6" block is 150% of the original. You cannot enlarge a block larger than 6", however, without making a copy from an enlarged copy, where the variance is already present. I don't recommend making copies of copies because the variance becomes greater with each generation of photocopies.

The Proportional Scale is a great tool for those who prefer not to make calculations. Just align the size of the original on the inner wheel with the desired size of the reduction or enlargement on the outer wheel, and the percentage of reduction or enlargement appears in the window!

Symmetrical and Asymmetrical Blocks

The 4" block designs represent the wrong side of the block. In a symmetrical design, the fabric side of the block design is the same as the marked side of the block. In an asymmetrical design, the fabric side of the block is the reverse of the marked side of the block. Use the block-front drawings and the color photographs to see how the blocks will appear from the front once they are pieced.

Symmetrical Geometric Block

Wrong side   Right side

Asymmetrical Boat Block

Wrong side   Right side

To reproduce the colors in a block-front drawing, simply indicate the color of the pieces on the blank side of the paper design to correspond with the finished color example. If you trace the blocks on tracing paper, the lines are easy to see. If you photocopy the blocks, the lines should be dark enough to see from the unmarked side when the paper is placed on a white surface. If they are not, simply place a light source beneath the block so the lines are more visible.

Creating the Reverse of a Block

There may be times when you actually do want to create the reverse of a block design. You could have your Ship blocks sailing off in different directions, or you might want to face two Doll blocks in opposite direc-

tions to create a wonderful new design. If you trace your blocks onto tracing paper, simply place the fabric pieces on the side with the pencil lines to create the reverse of the design. You'll be able to see the pencil lines through the paper, and sew without retracing the block. If you use a photocopy machine to reproduce your blocks, first trace the line design onto tracing paper with a dark pencil. Then, turn it over, retrace the lines, and mark the numbers on this side of the tracing paper. Mark the numbered side "reverse" so you won't become confused later. Copy the "reverse" design for your paper patterns.

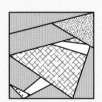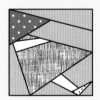

Original Design   Reversed Design

Cutting Fabric Pieces to Approximate Size

To cut fabric the approximate size for the intended area, take a quick measurement of the area with a ruler and add a total of ¾" to 1". You will cut the pieces a bit larger than necessary, as the customary seam allowance for patchwork is ¼". Trim the excess fabric to ¼" after sewing the adjoining seams. Since the line drawing that you measure is the wrong side of the block, always cut the fabric with the wrong side facing up. You can fill in unusual shapes with oversize rectangles or squares. You don't need to cut the exact shape.

Remember, when dealing with angled seams and odd shapes, bigger is always better. Before attaching these odd shapes, place the wrong side of the fabric on the blank side of the block, over the intended area. Hold the marked side of the foundation up to a light source and check to see that the cut piece of fabric is large enough to fill the intended area with a generous seam allowance all the way around. Since strips of fabric offer little placement variance, I tend to cut them the finished size plus ½" for the seam allowances.

Fabric Grain Options

Fabric has three grains: lengthwise, crosswise, and bias. The lengthwise grain has the least amount of stretch and runs parallel to the selvages. The crosswise grain runs from selvage to selvage and has a bit of stretch. Both the lengthwise and the crosswise grains are considered the straight grain of the fabric. The bias runs diagonally through the fabric and has the greatest amount of stretch.

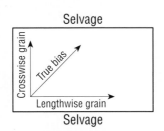

There are three choices for fabric-grain placement when piecing on paper foundations. You can piece the blocks with random-grain placement, straight-grain placement, or a combination of both.

Using Random-Grain Placement

With random-grain placement, the fabric pieces are sewn with no attention paid to the direction of the fabric grain along the sewing edge. This results in random grain direction when the piece is sewn and opened up. Paper piecing permits this type of random-grain piecing because the paper provides the stability necessary to prevent the pieces from stretching as they are sewn. However, bias edges along the edge of a block will stretch once the paper is removed. For this reason, I don't recommend using random-grain placement for block pieces at the outside edges of a project. It is also why I suggest that you do not remove the paper until the blocks have been joined to other blocks and/or borders.

Large pieces of fabric and directional-print fabric in random-grain placements can be distracting. Since fabric grain is more obvious in solid-color fabrics, use tiny-scale prints in place of solid-color fabrics to help hide random-grain directions.

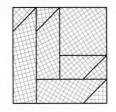

Random-grain placement

Using Straight-Grain Placement

In straight-grain placement, fabric pieces are positioned so that the straight of grain runs vertically and horizontally through the block. Straight-grain placement is important for block pieces at the outside edges of a project and when the fabric pieces are large enough to make the fabric grain noticeable.

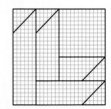

Straight-grain placement

It is not the shape of the fabric piece to be added that determines how the fabric piece is cut. Rather, it is the direction of the next seam to be sewn that determines how the fabric will be cut so it will open to the straight of grain.

Vertical and Horizontal Seam Lines

The Flag block is an example of a block that contains only vertical and horizontal lines. All the fabric strips and the rectangle should be cut on the straight grain of the fabric for straight-grain placement throughout the block.

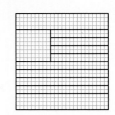

Straight-grain placement on vertical and horizontal lines

Diagonal Seam Lines

Fabrics that will be used on diagonal seam lines should be cut on the bias so that the vertical and horizontal sides of the block will both be on the straight grain of the fabric. In the Heart block example, the sewing edges of the pieces are all cut on the bias.

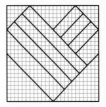

Bias-grain placement on diagonal lines

To cut fabric on the bias, cut strips diagonally at a 45° angle.

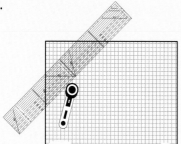

Sewing "Weird" Angle Seams

Weird-grain fabric edges are placed on weird angles. I use the term "weird" for any seam line that is not horizontal, vertical, or at a 45° angle. I use this term only because it is not necessary to know what the angle is, only how to cut the fabric so that it will end up on the straight grain once it is sewn and opened. Use the following method to cut weird angles so they finish on the straight of grain:

1. Place the block design on the cutting mat.
2. Place a long rotary ruler along the seam line you are about to sew—the "weird" angle.
3. Place the fabric you intend to add, wrong side up, either above or below the block and under the extending end of the ruler; cut the angle with a rotary cutter. Make sure the straight grain of the fabric runs vertically and horizontally.

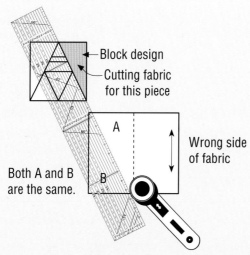

Block design
Cutting fabric for this piece
A
Wrong side of fabric
Both A and B are the same.
B

4. To avoid possible confusion, cut weird-angle pieces as you need them. I like to make a small pencil mark on the paper block of the weird-angle piece I just cut so that I don't forget.
5. Place the cut edge of the fabric along the seam; sew in place and open.

To cut the reverse of a weird angle, fold the fabric right sides together and cut both layers at the same time.

Remember that when cutting bias pieces and weird angles, bigger is better. Oversize pieces ensure that the fabric fills the intended area once it is sewn and opened. You can always trim the excess fabric after sewing the adjoining pieces. When making multiples of the same block design, use the cut fabric piece as a template to cut the additional pieces from a strip of fabric.

When the first piece of a block contains weird angles, simply pin the piece right side up with the straight grain going vertically and horizontally.

Placing Fabric Strips

Several block designs require strips of fabric. Use straight-grain strips when the strips are sewn vertically or horizontally in the block. You can also use straight-grain strips along diagonal seams if you piece with random-grain placement. Cut bias strips for diagonally-sewn strips so that edges finish on the straight of grain.

You can precut a supply of fabric strips on the bias or on the straight of grain to the finished width plus ½" for seam allowances. Add straight-grain fabric strips to any of the paper block designs to enlarge them or to stabilize the outside edges where you used random-grain fabric placement.

Straight grain placement on vertical and horizontal seam lines.

Straight grain strips placed on diagonal seam lines will yield bias grain at the edge of the block.

Bias grain strips placed on diagonal seam lines will yield straight grain at the edge of the block.

As you can see, there are several options for fabric-grain placement when paper piecing. Don't become overwhelmed. Deal with fabric grain on a block-by-block basis at first, and your options and choices will become clear.

Quilt Blocks

This portion of the book contains the mechanics of sewing paper-pieced blocks. There is much more information presented than you need to get started. Since the best way to learn is by doing, begin by piecing small blocks with random-grain placement to practice cutting and sewing the fabric pieces. Then move on to the larger blocks and straight-grain placement. As you create the blocks, the techniques will become second nature. When you need a refresher, you can always refer to this section in the book.

Getting Ready to Sew

Whenever I begin a project, I set the stage so that I have everything I am going to need at my fingertips. Getting up and down for needed items may provide exercise, but it slows your progress.

- Make sure that your sewing machine is in working order and sews a good straight stitch.
- Set the stitch length on your machine for approximately 18 to 20 stitches per inch. A short stitch length perforates the paper better, which makes it easier to tear away later.
- Use a size 90/14 needle; the larger needle also helps perforate the paper.
- Select a sewing thread that blends with most of the fabrics used.
- Create a pressing and cutting area next to the machine by lowering the ironing board to sewing level; use one end to cut and the other end to press.
- Have a sharp pair of small scissors handy to trim the fabric pieces before and after you sew them.
- Keep your rotary cutter, acrylic ruler, and mat close at hand. Choose the ruler size based on the size of the blocks being made.
- Have your "unsewing" tool (seam ripper) handy just on the outside chance that a quick take-out maneuver becomes necessary.
- Set up a small lamp near the sewing machine. Generally, the fabric placement of the first piece is easy to see without a light source. However, to place subsequent pieces of fabric, you need to see through the previous pieces of untrimmed fabric.
- Last, but probably most important, select your fabric. Remember, the unmarked side of the block is the fabric side. To avoid confusion, always note your fabric choices on the unmarked side of the block design.

Tip: When using larger pieces of fabric (rather than scraps), cut strips approximately 6" wide; then, cut smaller pieces from the strips as needed. This makes the fabric more manageable and the sewing area less cluttered.

Now you are all set to begin paper piecing. You might want to put on some upbeat or relaxing music and make yourself that favorite cup of tea. This is going to be fun!

Step-by-Step Sewing Procedure

1. Place the fabric for piece #1, right side up, on the unmarked side of the paper; pin in place. Make sure piece #1 covers the area marked 1 and extends a generous ¼" on all sides. You can cut the piece larger than needed and trim the excess fabric after the adjoining seams are sewn. Once you have sewn a few blocks, you may want to eliminate the pin and just hold the first piece in position. If using photocopies, hold the paper up to a light source with the marked side of the block toward you, to facilitate proper placement.

2. With the wrong side of the fabric facing you, cut the approximate size of piece #2. Remember, the marked side of the block is the wrong side of the block. Place piece #2 on top of piece #1, right sides

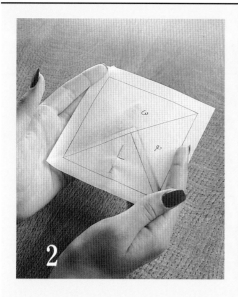

2

3

4

together, along the joining seam line; make sure both fabrics extend at least ¼" beyond the seam lines. Don't concern yourself with an exact ¼"-wide seam allowance. You can trim any excess seam allowance after the seam is sewn. However, you do want to keep the edge of piece #2 parallel to the seam line to keep the grain true.

Tip: Check to make sure the piece is placed correctly and is large enough by holding the seam-allowance edge and opening piece #2 to see if it covers the intended area plus seam allowances.

3. Holding the fabrics in place, lay the paper block with the marked side up under the presser foot and sew the first seam line between pieces #1 and #2.

Extend the stitching a few stitches beyond the beginning and the end of the line.

4. Trim away any excess fabric in the seam allowance to ¼". Open piece #2 and fingerpress by running your fingers across the seam. Press with an iron on a cotton setting with no steam.

5. Add piece #3 across the first two pieces. Sew the second seam line between #1/#2 and piece #3.

6. Using a rotary cutter and ruler, trim the edges of the block, leaving a ¼"-wide seam allowance beyond the outside lines of the marked design. If the ruler slips on the paper, apply small circular stick-on tabs of sandpaper to stabilize it.

No matter how many pieces a block design has, the construction is the same. Always add pieces in numerical order until the design is complete.

5

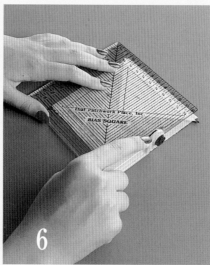

6

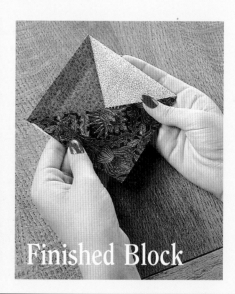

Finished Block

Alternative Method for Placing Fabrics

Instead of using a light source to place subsequent fabric pieces, you can trim the previously sewn fabric(s) ¼" beyond the next line you are going to sew to create an accurate placement for the next piece. To do this, fold the lined side of the paper back on itself along the next sewing line. To make this easier, place a very thin ruler or a 3" x 5" card on the line and fold the paper back at the edge of the card or ruler. Place the rotary ruler's ¼" line on the fold and trim any excess fabric ¼" from the fold. Now the next piece of fabric to be joined can be placed flush along this trimmed fabric edge. You simply trim away the excess fabric before the seam is sewn rather than afterward.

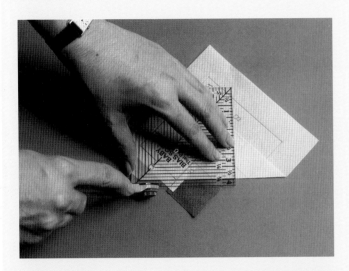

Sewing Tips

- Whenever possible, stitch in the direction of the points. This makes it easy to see that you are crossing the other line of stitching at the desired location.

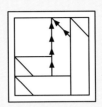

Stitch in the direction of points when possible.

- Use an open-front presser foot on your machine for best visibility. If your sewing machine has a knee lift for the presser foot, use it. The knee lift lowers the feed dogs as it raises the presser foot and allows the positioned fabrics to slip under the presser foot easily.
- If you need several half-square triangles, cut over-size squares (finished short side of the triangle plus 1¼") and cut once diagonally.

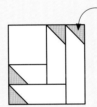

Finished size: 1"
Cut 2 squares 2¼" x 2¼" to yield 4 half-square triangles.

- If you need several quarter-square triangles, cut oversize squares (finished long side of the triangle plus 1½") and cut twice diagonally.

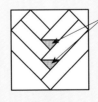

Finished size of long side of triangle is 1". Cut 1 square 2½" and cut twice diagonally to yield 4 quarter-square triangles.

- When trimming seam allowances, fold the paper back slightly so it will not interfere.
- Use tracing paper when you want to center a design on the first piece of fabric you place. The design is easy to see through the tracing paper.
- For better control, hold the paper on both sides while sewing.

- When adding straight-grain strips to the outside edges of several blocks that will be joined, alternate the long pieces from the top and bottom edges to the sides so you won't have to match the seam intersections.

- When your iron is not close at hand, fingerpress each seam to quickly crease the pieces.
- Always overestimate the size of the pieces; you can trim away the excess. Remember, bigger is better!
- Since it is difficult to see from the reverse side whether you are sewing along the straight grain of striped or checked fabrics, you may want to choose fabrics that do not have a directional print.
- In areas where lots of seams come together, use a dark fabric to cover the seam allowances.
- If you open the fabric and the piece doesn't quite meet at a perfect point, simply sew again, taking a deeper seam.
- Cut the excess threads after sewing each seam.
- If the project calls for multiple blocks in identical fabrics, make one block to confirm your fabric choices; then make the remainder of the blocks in assembly-line fashion, adding the same piece to each block before adding the next piece.
- If you can't trim the seam allowances to ¼" because of cross-seam stitching, simply lift the seam to pull the stitching away from the paper.
- Consider using the wrong side of the fabric as the right side. Often, it appears as a lighter-colored version of the print or as a solid.
- Iron delicate fabrics, such as lamés and silks, by pressing from the paper side once the piece has been opened. If you use copies from a photocopy machine, protect your iron from the ink, which may transfer onto a hot iron, by using a scrap pressing cloth. For the same reason, use a pressing cloth to protect your ironing board when pressing blocks on the right side.

Making Two-Section Blocks

The Dove, Nosegay, Apple, Angel, and Christmas Light blocks are two-section blocks. That means you piece the two sections of the block as if they were separate blocks, trim ¼" from the adjoining seam lines, and then join the two sections to form the square. I have found that it saves time to machine baste about an inch across any matching points first, to ensure a good match before stitching the two sections. Once you've sewn the two sections together, press the joining seam open to reduce bulk, and trim the block ¼" beyond the outside seam line as usual.

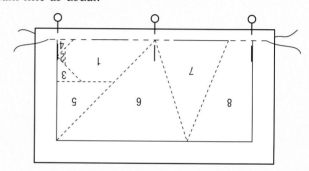

Pin and machine baste the two completed sections at important matching points.

The finished Dove block

Making Pieced Units

Adding pieced units expands the design possibilities. A pieced unit is noted by a "//" mark through the prepieced seam, and the unit is assigned a number in the sequence.

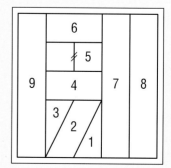

Single Straight-Seam Units

The Letter R block shows how the #5 piece is prepieced to make one unit. To determine the cut size of the fabric needed, measure the sizes of the squares and add ½" to ¾" for seam allowances. The squares measure a bit more than ¾", so you can cut a square 1½" x 1½" from the background and from the letter fabric. Sew the two squares together with the standard ¼"-wide seam allowance. Press the seam allowance to the darker side. When it is time to add the #5 piece, position the seam along the seam line on the paper. Sew the #5 piece in place and trim any excess fabric after the adjoining pieces have been sewn, or use the alternative placement method described on page 11.

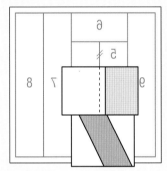

The letter "R" as seen from the blank side of the block with the prepieced strip placed in position.

Double Straight-Seam Units

Several of the Tree blocks require a pieced unit with two straight seams. The Tree block is used as an example; however, the same information holds true for any paper-pieced block that has two straight prepieced seams. If making only one unit, cut the trunk strip the finished measurement plus ½" for seam allowances. Cut two pieces of background fabric the finished measurement plus ½" for seam allowances. Piece the three pieces together with the trunk fabric in the center; join to the bottom of the tree as one unit, aligning the seam lines with the drawing.

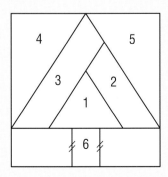

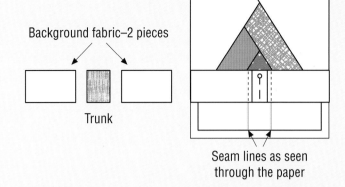

Background fabric—2 pieces

Trunk

Seam lines as seen through the paper

When making several Tree blocks, cut the strips the correct width and long enough to accommodate the number of units needed. For example, the bottom strip of this Tree block is 1" finished. Add ½" for seam allowances. If you need ten units, multiply 1½" by 10, and cut each strip 15" long. Cut 1 strip for the trunk, 1¼" x 15"; cut 2 strips for the background, each 2⅛" x 15". Sew the trunk strip between 2 background strips; then cut the pieced strip into 1½"-wide units and attach them to the bottoms of the blocks.

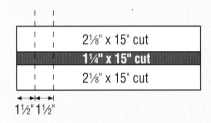

2⅛" x 15" cut
1¼" x 15" cut
2⅛" x 15" cut
1½" 1½"

Using a Second Paper Foundation to Create Pieced Units

When pieced units involve weird-angle units or units not easily measured with a ruler, use a second foundation to prepiece these units. Trim the pieced unit to ¼" from the adjoining seam, tear it away from this second foundation, and place it in position as a pieced unit. You can reproduce the entire block or just that portion of the block that involves the pieced section. If making multiples of the block, trace the pieced unit portion several times or photocopy the tracings.

Prepiecing the unit on a second foundation was my solution for the design challenge presented by the Letter X block. To make the Letter X block, make two paper foundations. One foundation will be the entire block design. The second foundation can be another copy of the entire block or a tracing of just the pieced unit (#5a, #5b, and #5c). Piece fabrics in the #1 through #4 positions on the full block foundation. Trim the excess fabric ¼" from the #4 seam, using the alternative method for placing fabrics described on page 11. On the other foundation, piece the three fabric pieces in the #5a, #5b, and #5c positions. Trim the excess fabric ¼" from the #4 seam, using the alternative method again. Now tear the foundation away from this second unit (composed of the #5 pieces), and position it as a pieced unit on the first foundation, flush with the edge of the #4 fabric. Use pins to position the cross seams correctly on the foundation and sew. Complete the block with pieces #6 and #7.

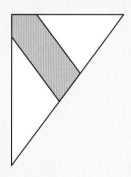 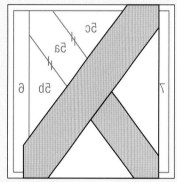

The #6 unit in the Letter B block has several prepieced squares that are not easily measured. Prepiece the #6a through #6e fabrics on a second foundation, trim along the #4/#2 line as described above, and place in position as a pieced unit.

Block Designs

The designs have been grouped in the following categories:

Geometrics	G19, G27–G30
Flowers/Hearts/Basket	F27–F31
	B12
	H8, H11, H12
Trees	T9–T14
Pictures	P14–P27
Christmas	C1–C12
Letters	L1–L26

Rather than name each of the block designs as is normally the case in patchwork, I have assigned letters and numbers for reference purposes as I did in *Easy Machine Paper Piecing* and *Easy Reversible Vests*. All these designs will work with the blocks in those books, which expands the design possibilities even further.

Geometric block G19 and Heart block H8 can also be found in *Easy Reversible Vests* in a 3" size. All the other block designs are new to this book.

Block Photos

The blocks shown on pages 52–59 are only suggestions for fabric placement in the finished blocks. There are many other options that will yield different patchwork looks from the same line drawing. Individual photographs are not shown for the Letter blocks because they are simply pieced as shaded. The Sampler Quilt on page 66 contains the entire alphabet.

4" Block Designs

You can trace, photocopy, enlarge, or reduce the block designs to create quilt blocks. The lines on the block design represent the sewing lines, and the numbers represent the piecing sequence. Using paper piecing to make blocks is quick; however, a block with five pieces is still quicker to piece than a block with seventeen pieces. A block that has more pieces or tinier pieces is no more difficult to piece than a block with a few large pieces. It will only take more time.

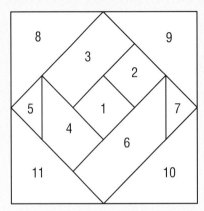

4" Block Design (stitching side)

The 4" block design represents the wrong side of the block. This is of no consequence for symmetrical blocks. However, asymmetrical blocks result in the reverse pattern on the finished side.

Block designs that have several merging seams at one corner are shown with an optional seam variation, which is indicated with a dotted line. See page 68 for more information about added seam variations.

Block-Front Drawings

These small drawings show how the finished blocks will appear from the fabric side. They can be photocopied and used for quilt-design purposes. You can also make quilt layout work sheets to help you create your own quilt layouts. See "Quilt Layouts" on page 70. Arrange the blocks in several settings and in conjunction with other blocks or fabric squares and borders until you have created a pleasing design. Once you are satisfied with your layout, photocopy the design layout several times and use colored pencils to try different color schemes. Use the block-front drawings to make your design and color selection, and note your choices on the unmarked sides of the corresponding 4" block designs.

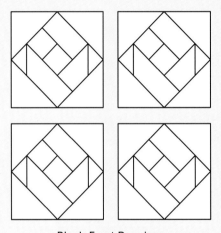

Block-Front Drawings

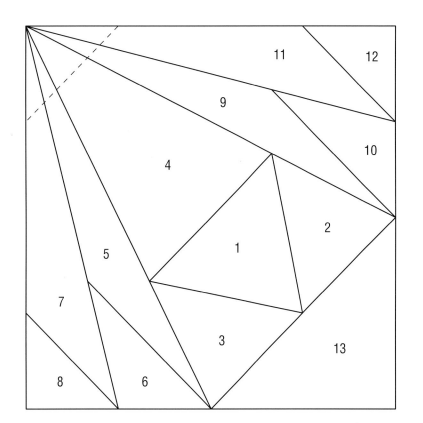

G19

Color photo: page 52

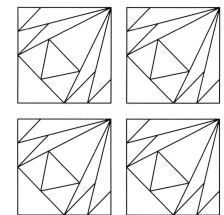

G27

Color photo: page 52

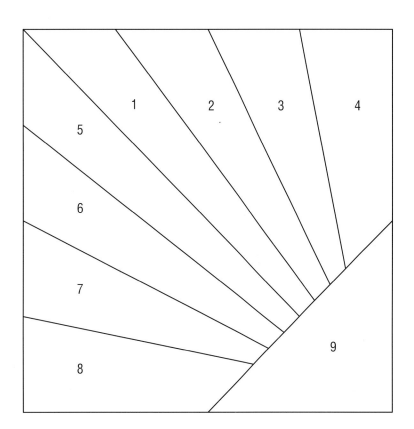

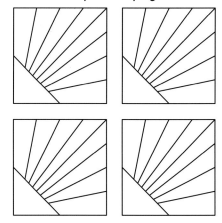

G28
Color photo: page 52

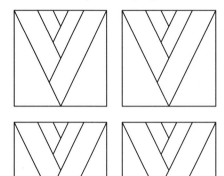

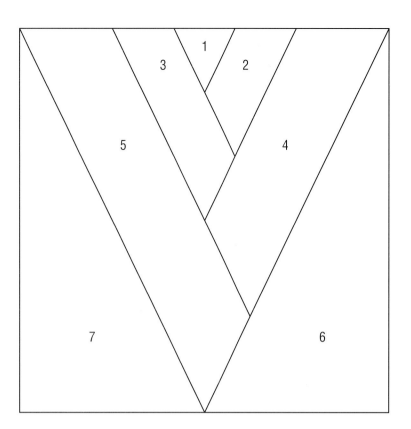

G29
Color photo: page 52

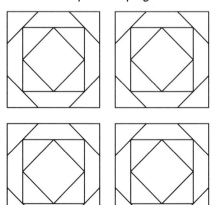

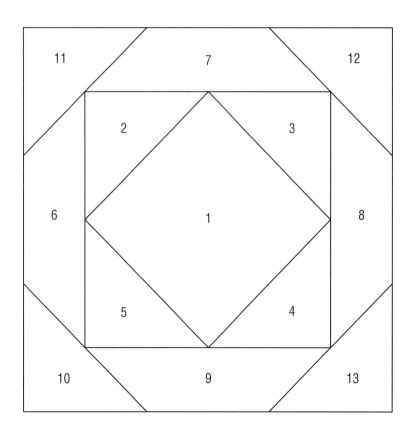

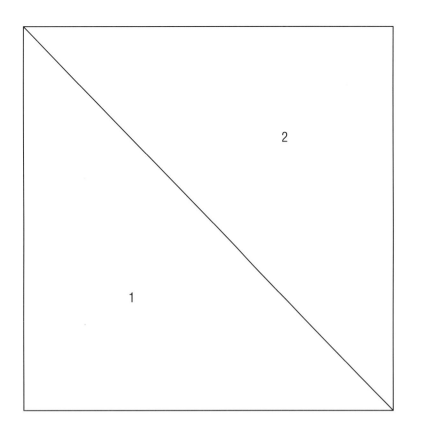

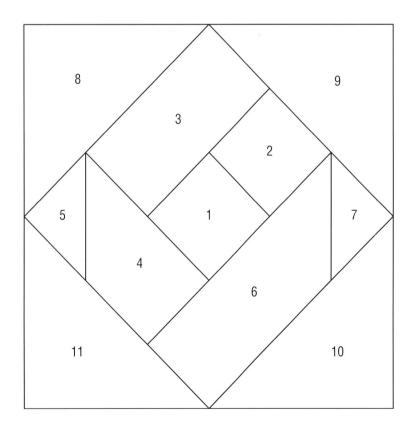

G30
Color photo: page 52

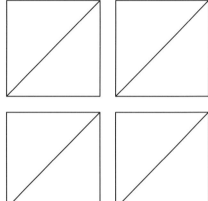

Flower, Heart, & Basket Blocks

F27
Color photo: page 53

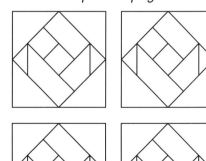

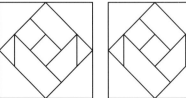

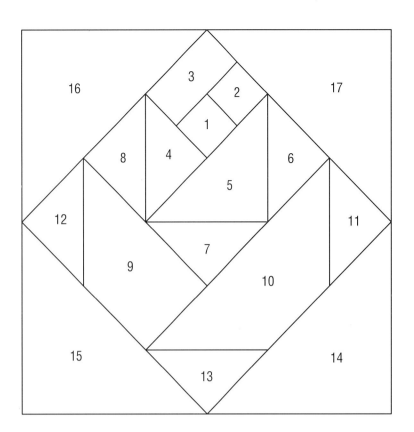

F28

Color photo: page 53

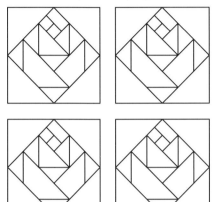

F29

Color photo: page 53

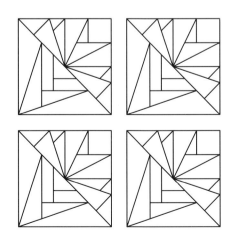

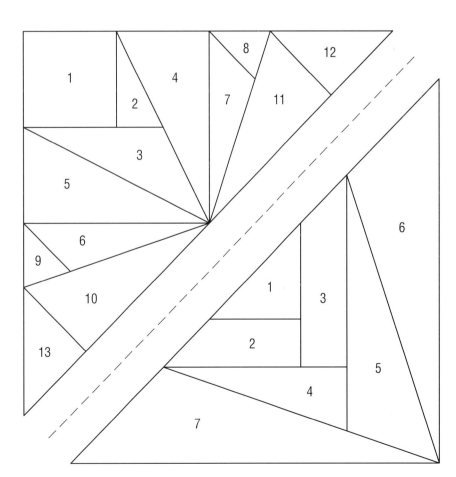

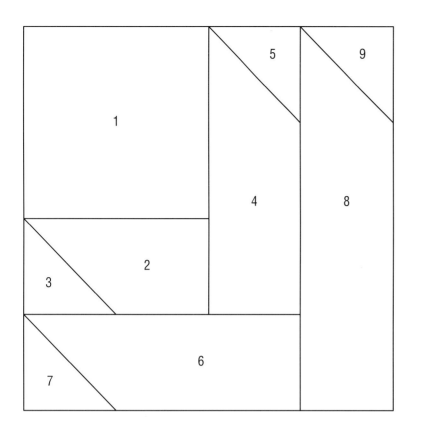

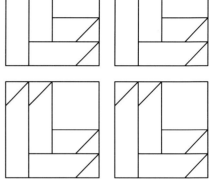

F30

Color photo: page 53

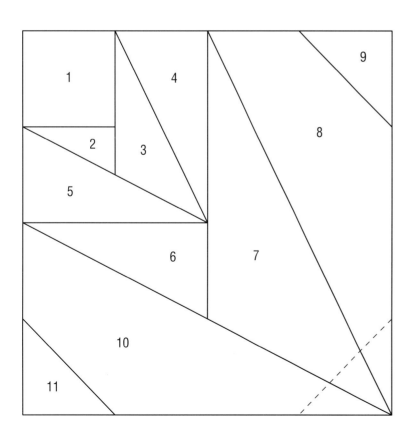

F31

Color photo: page 53

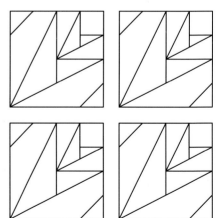

B12

Color photo: page 53

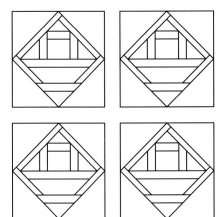

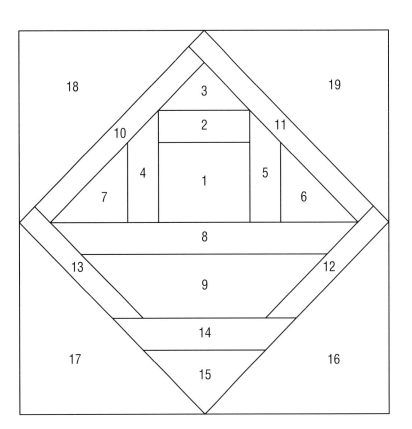

H8

Color photo: page 54

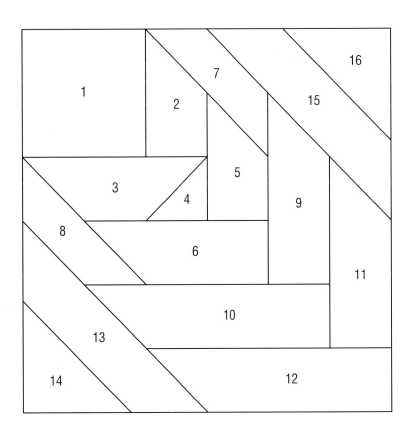

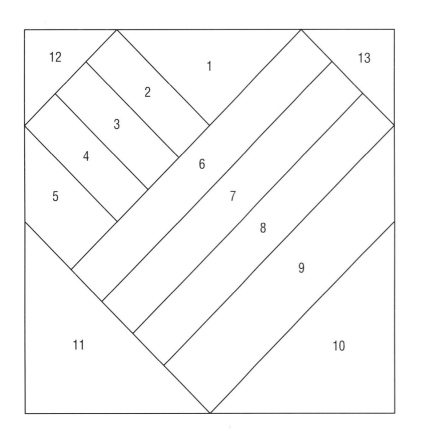

H11

Color photo: page 54

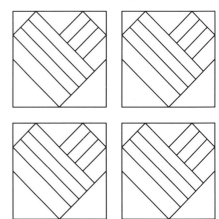

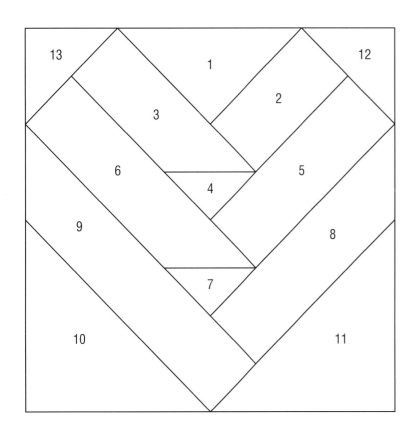

H12

Color photo: page 54

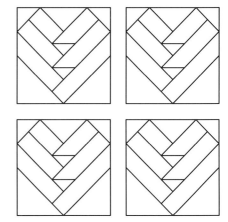

Tree Blocks

T9

Color photo: page 59

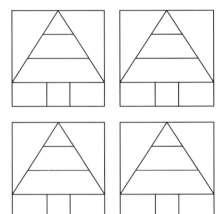

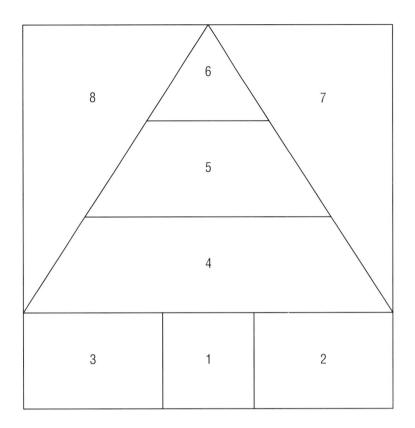

T10

Color photo: page 59

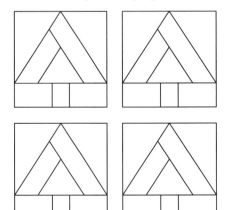

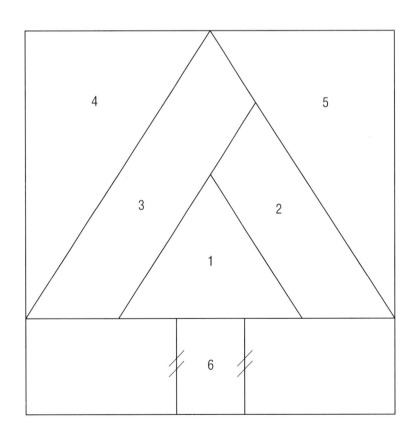

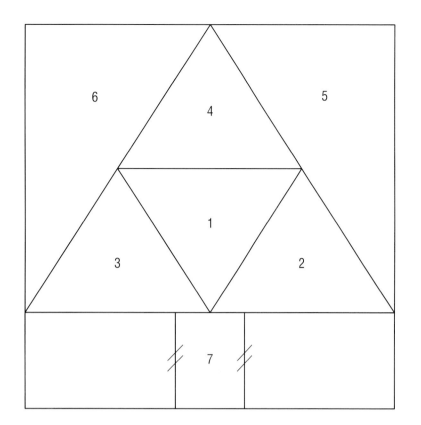

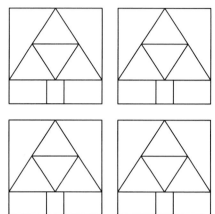

T11
Color photo: page 59

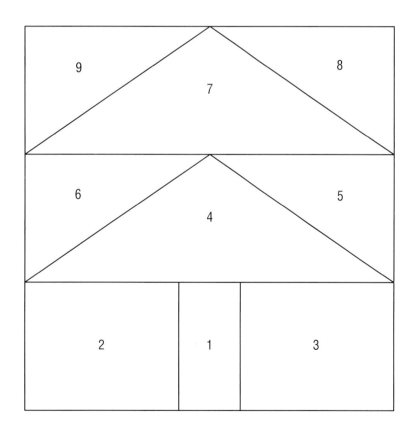

T12
Color photo: page 59

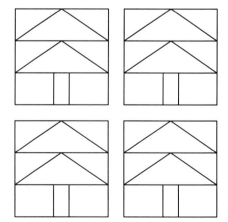

T13
Color photo: page 59

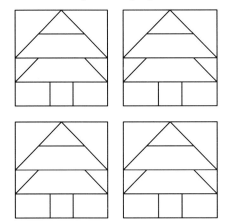

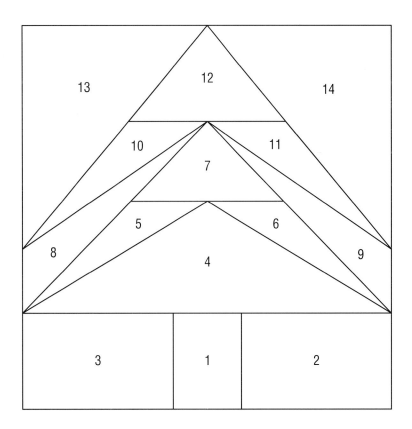

T14
Color photo: page 59

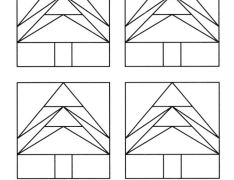

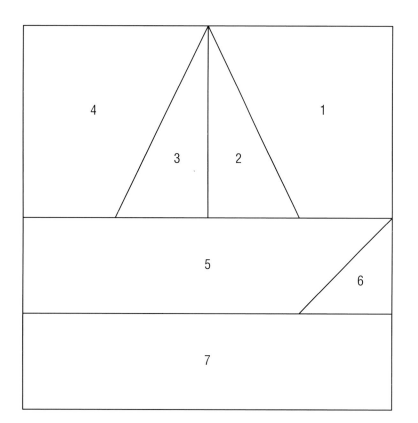

P14
Color photo: page 54

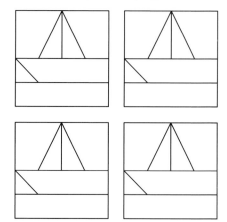

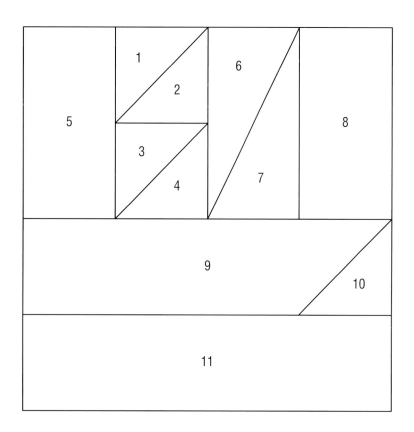

P15
Color photo: page 54

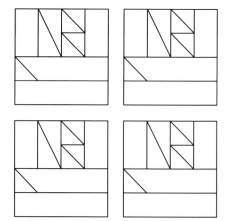

P16

Color photo: page 55

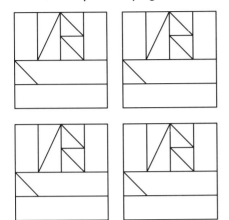

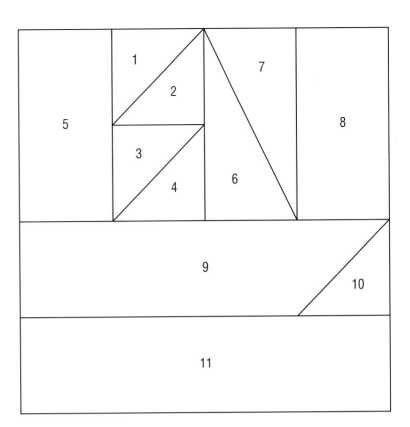

P17

Color photo: page 55

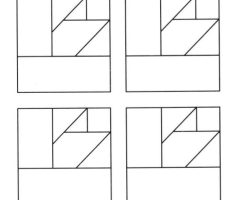

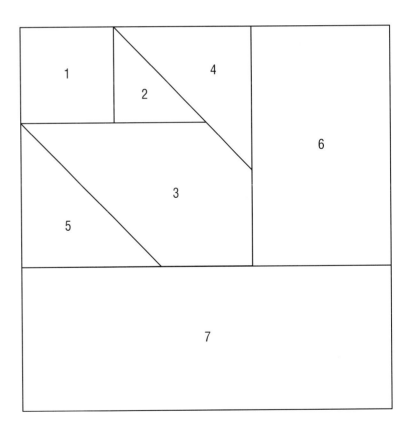

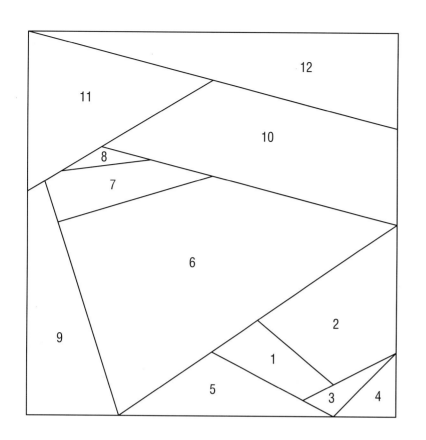

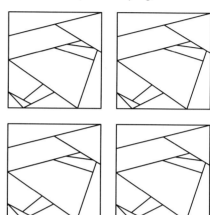

P18

Color photo: page 55

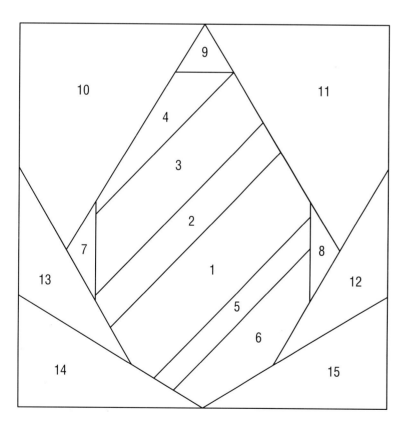

P19

Color photo: page 55

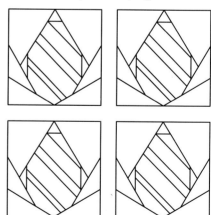

P20

Color photo: page 55

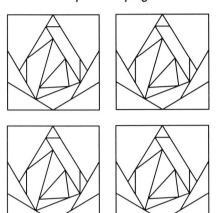

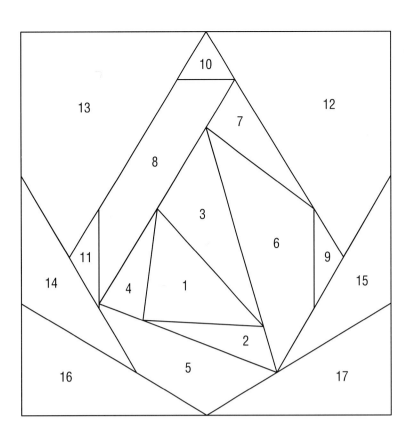

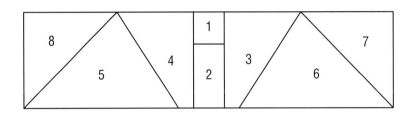

P21

Color photo: page 55

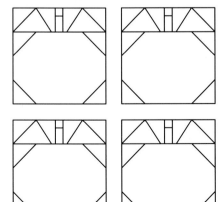

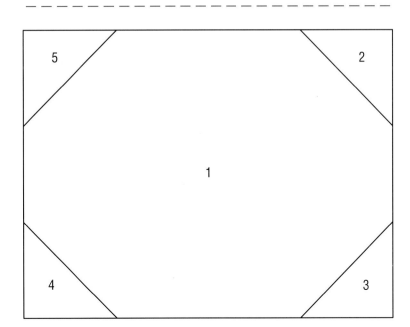

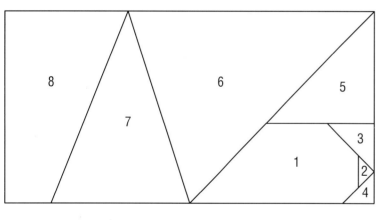

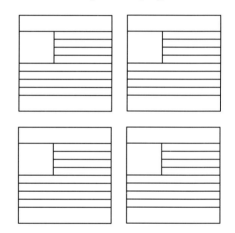

P22

Color photo: page 56

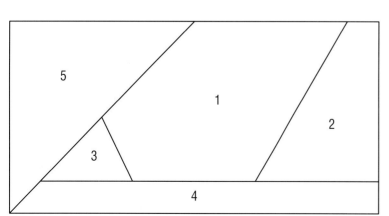

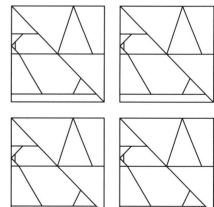

P23

Color photo: page 56

P24

Color photo: page 56

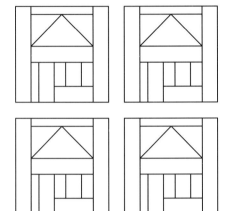

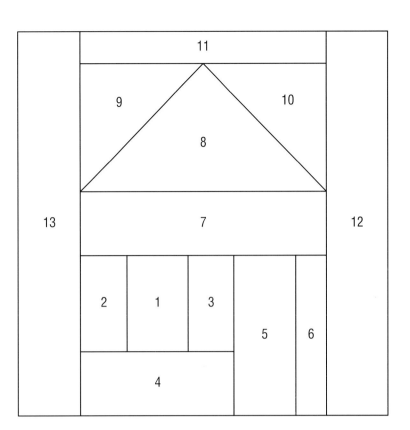

P25

Color photo: page 56

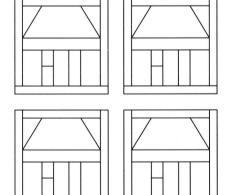

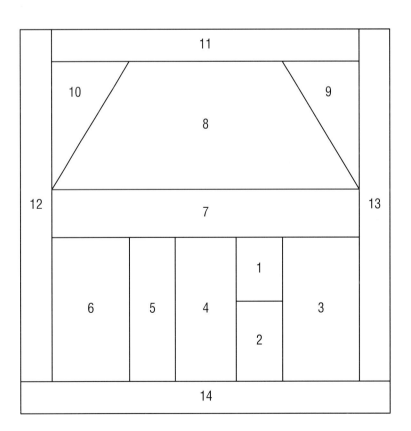

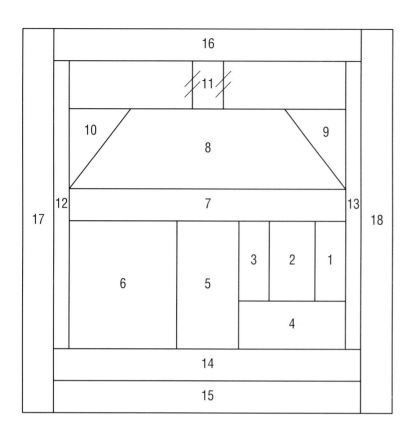

P26

Color photo: page 56

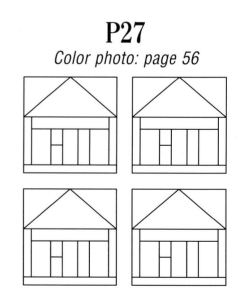

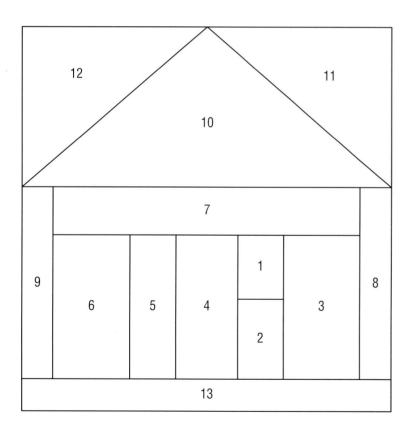

P27

Color photo: page 56

Christmas Blocks

C1

Color photo: page 57

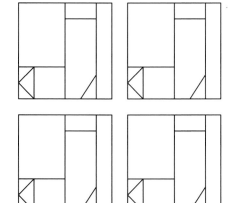

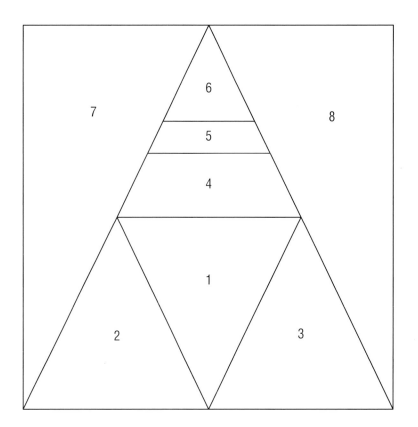

C2

Color photo: page 57

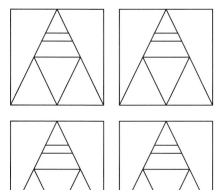

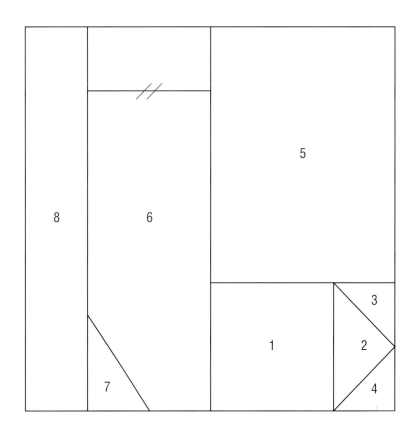

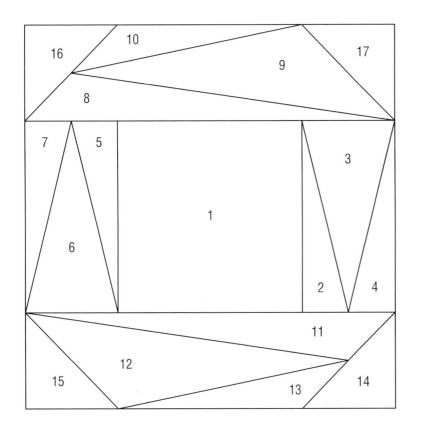

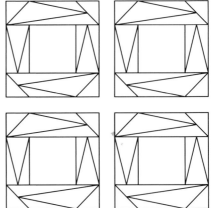

C3

Color photo: page 57

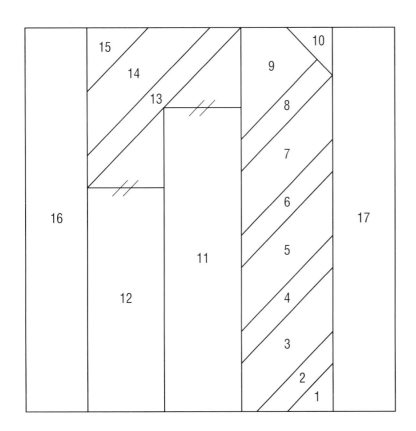

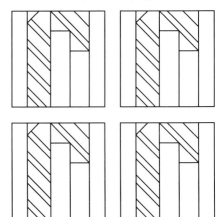

C4

Color photo: page 57

C5
Color photo: page 57

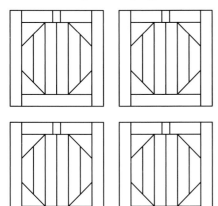

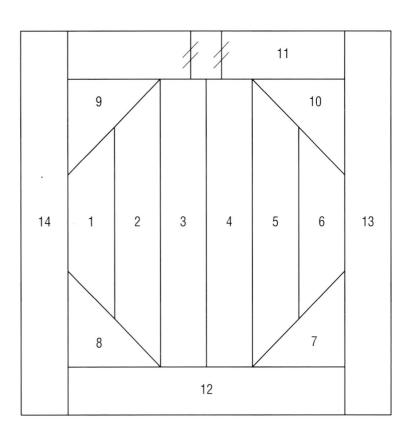

C6
Color photo: page 57

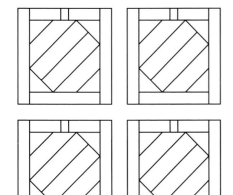

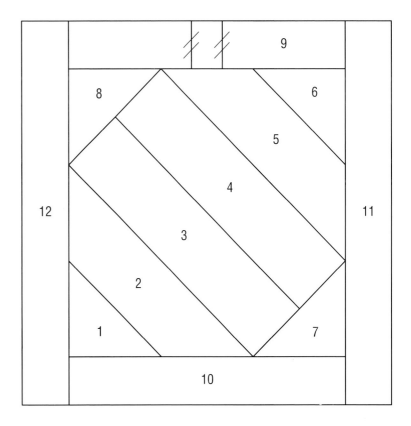

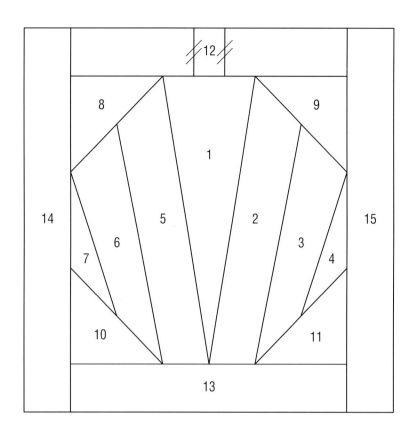

C7

Color photo: page 58

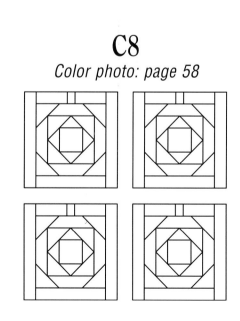

C8

Color photo: page 58

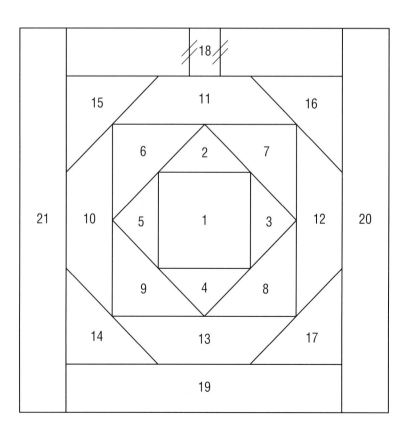

C9

Color photo: page 58

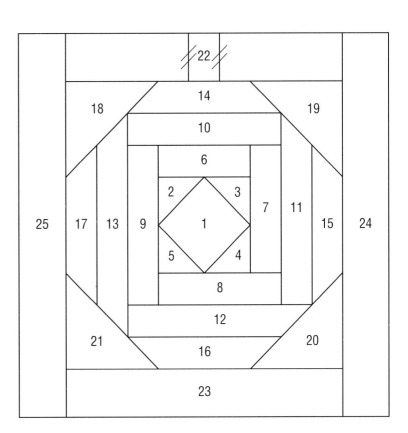

C10

Color photo: page 58

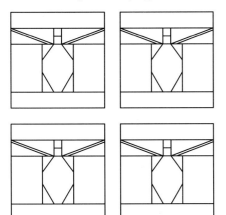

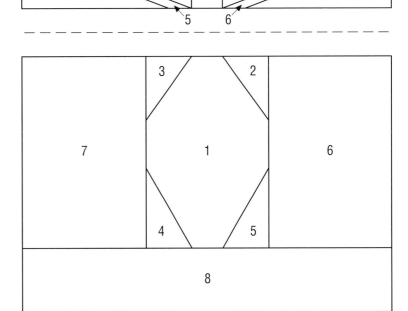

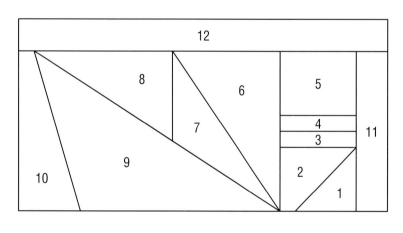

C11
Color photo: page 58

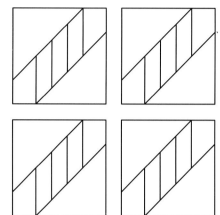

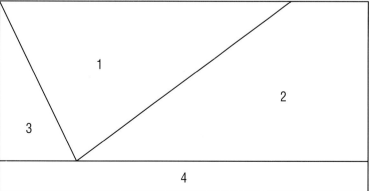

C12
Color photo: page 58

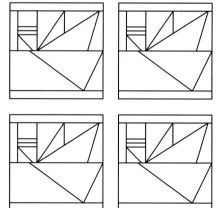

Block Designs

Letter Blocks

For color examples of the Letter blocks see the photo of the Sampler Quilt on page 66.

L1

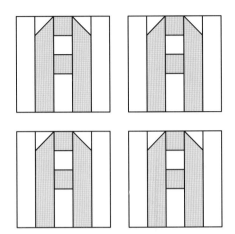

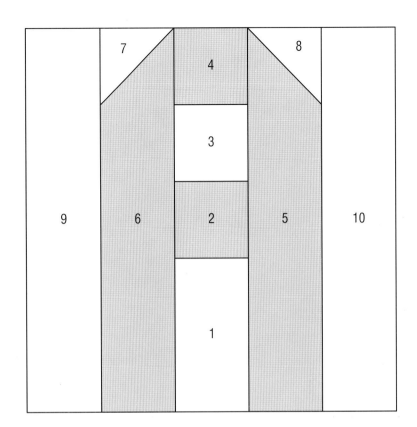

L2

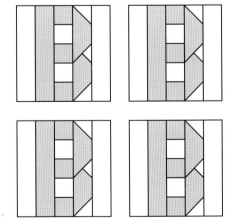

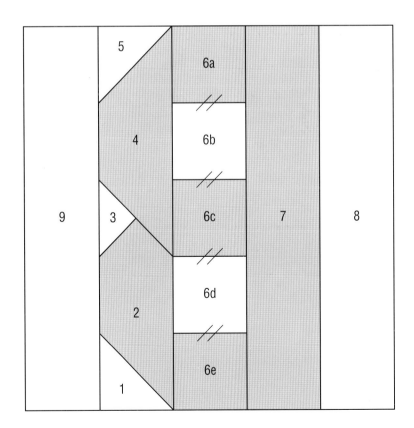

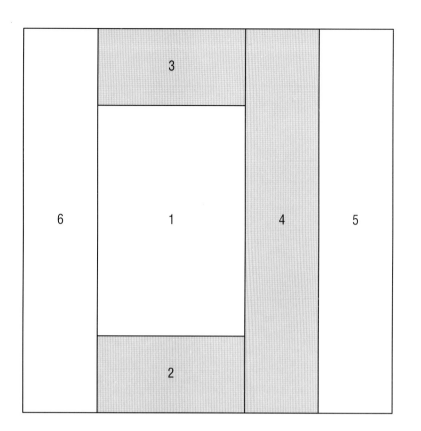

L3

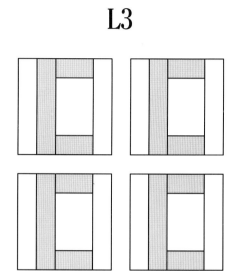

L4

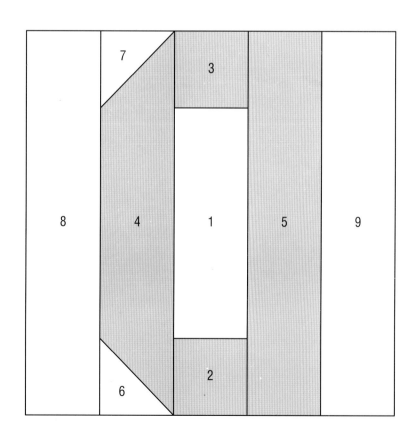

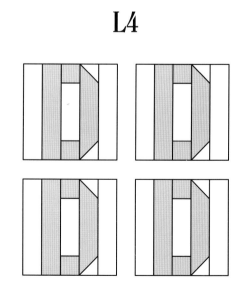

L5

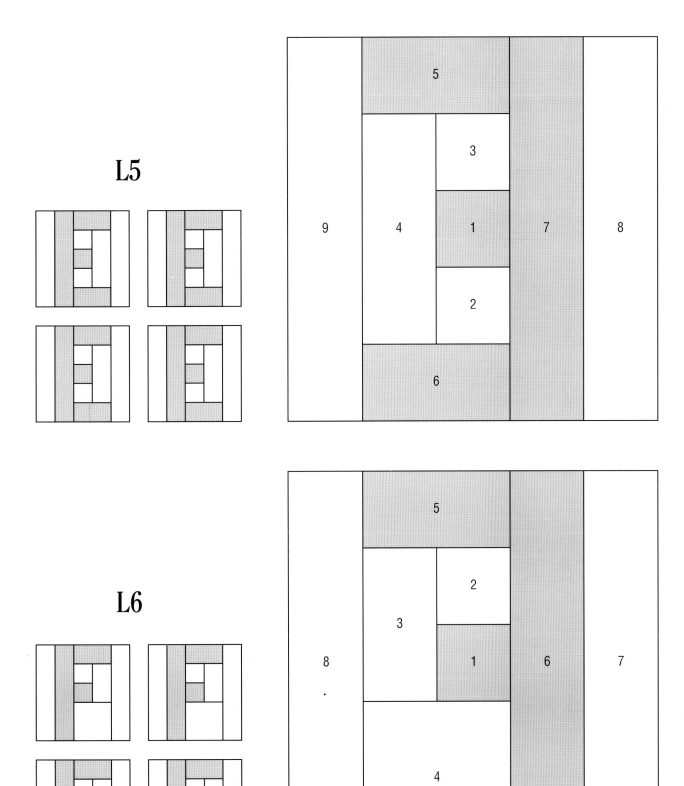

L6

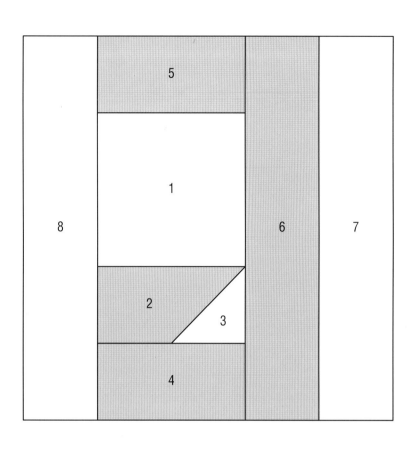

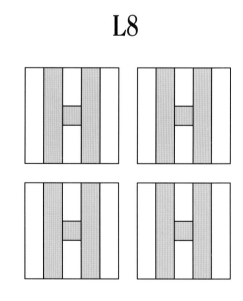

L7

L8

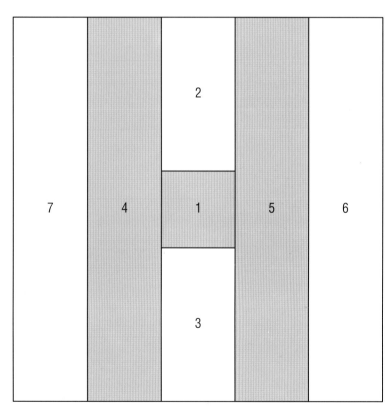

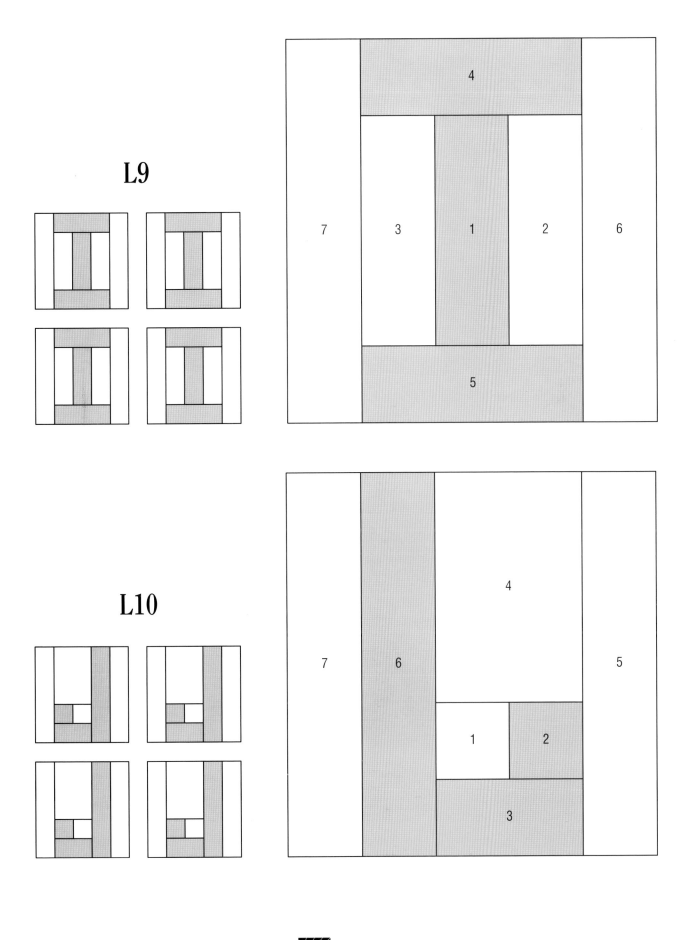

L9

L10

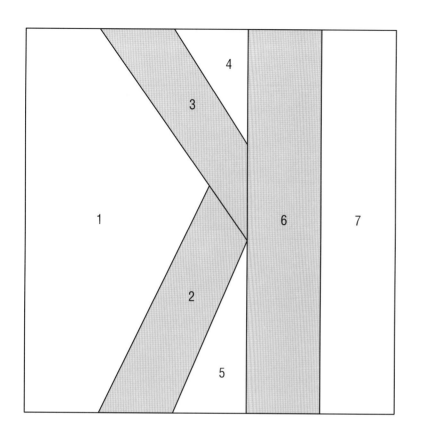

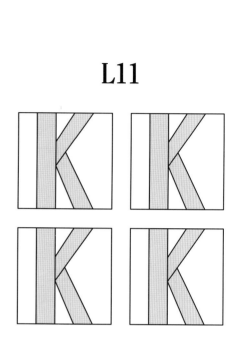

L11

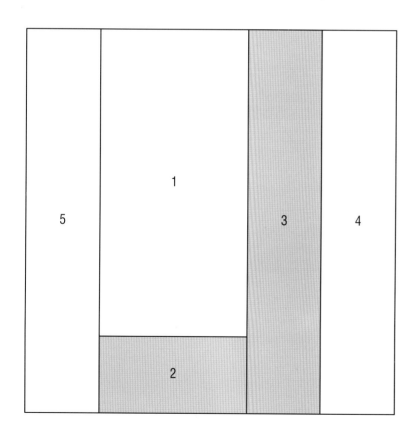

L12

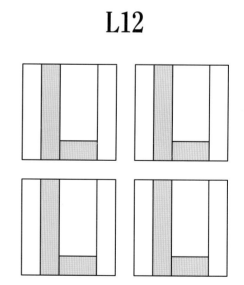

Block Designs

L13

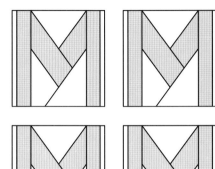

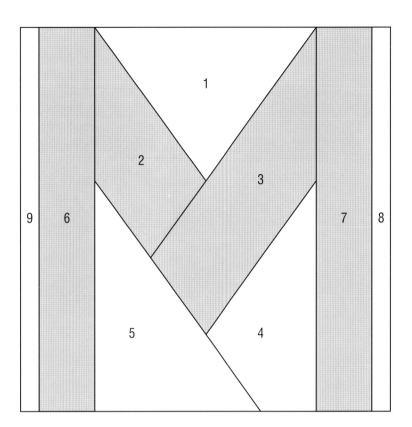

L14

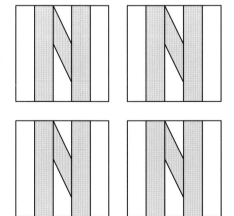

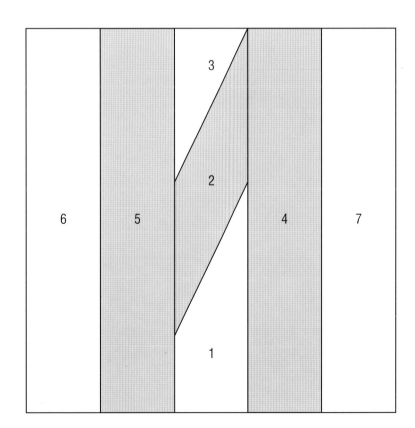

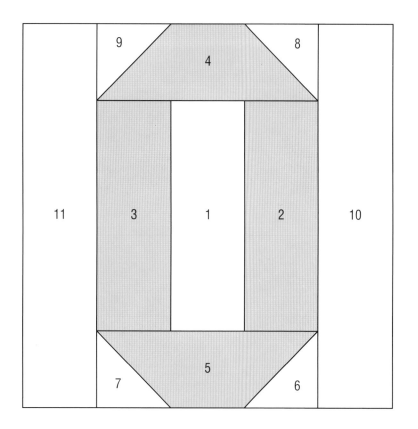

L15

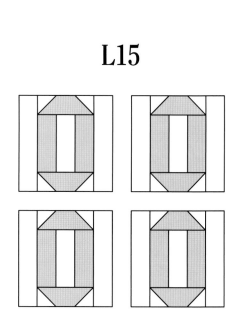

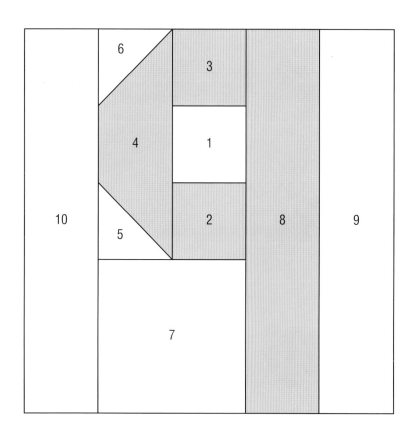

L16

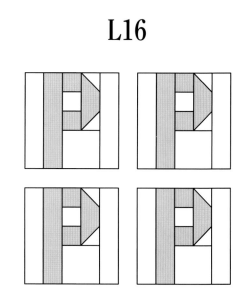

L17

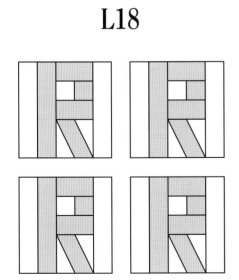

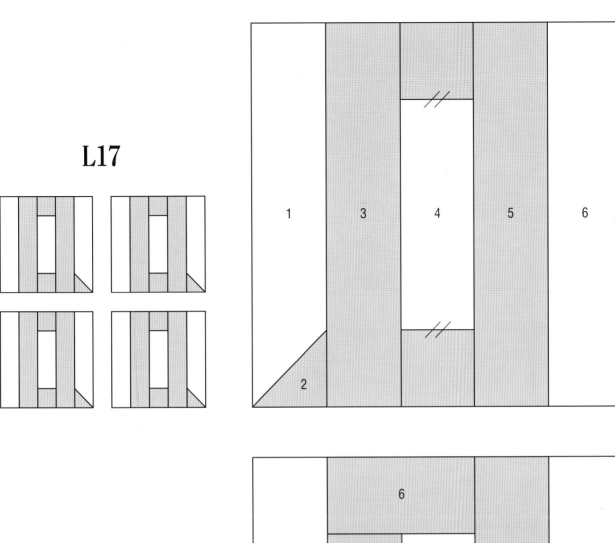

L18

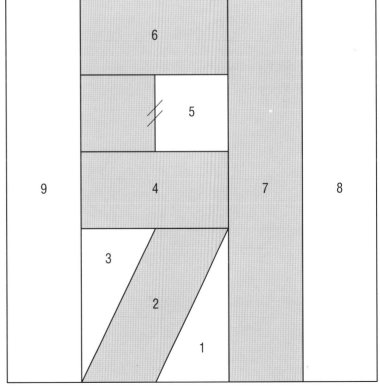

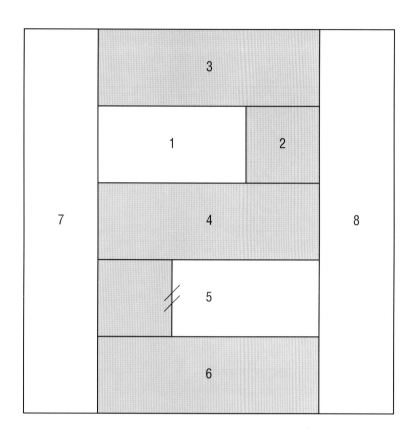

L19

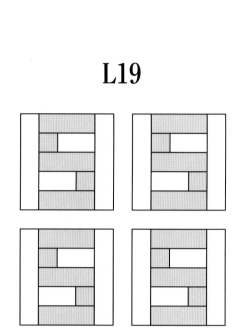

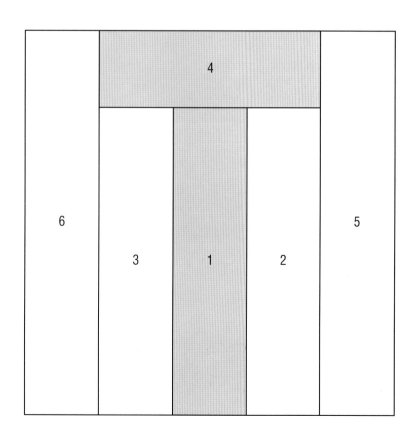

L20

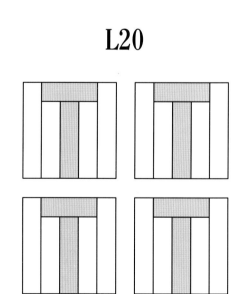

L21

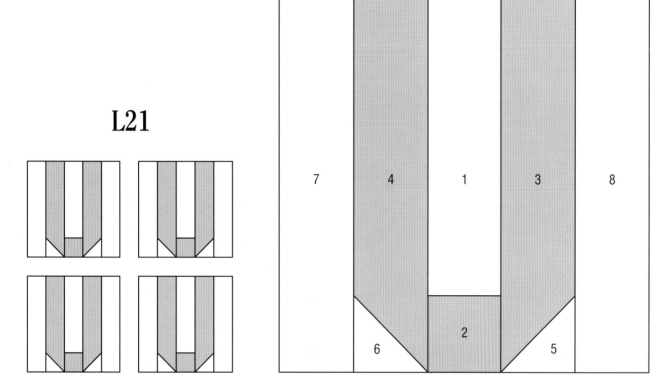

L22

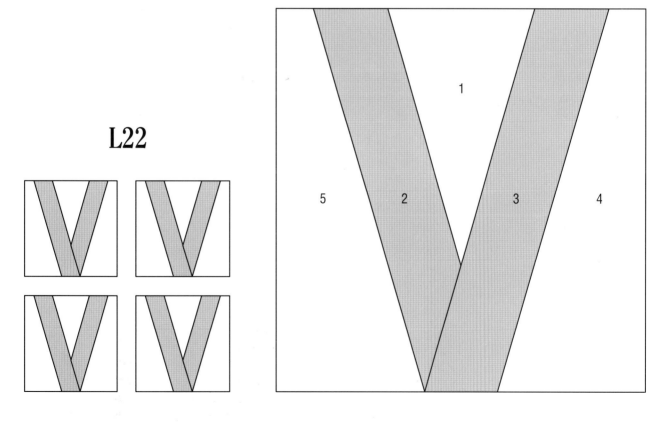

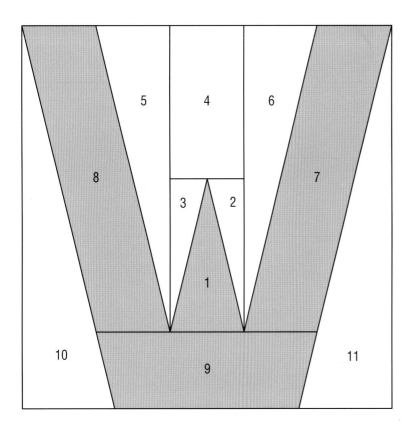

L23

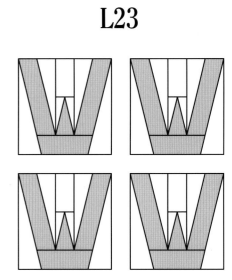

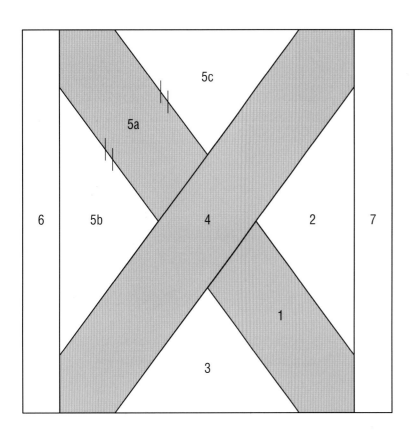

L24

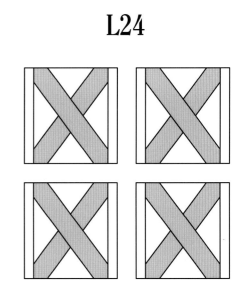

Block Designs

L25

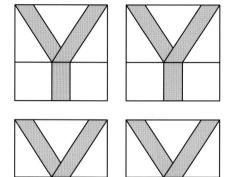

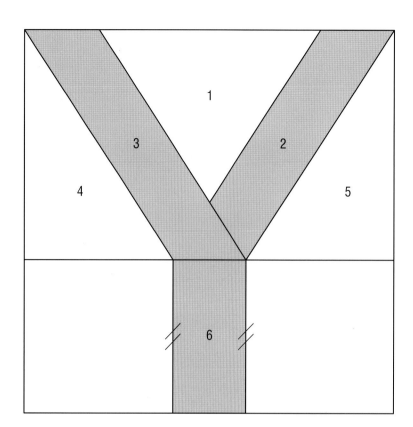

L26

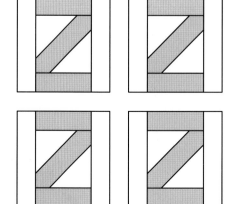

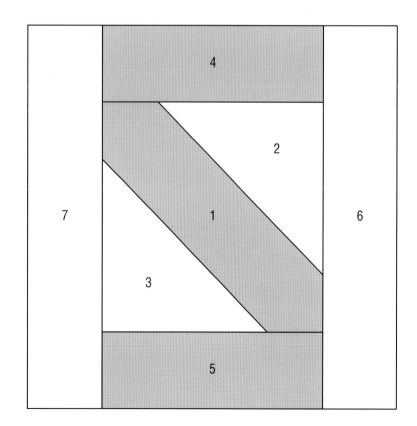

Geometric Blocks

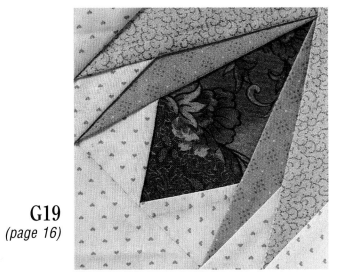

G19
(page 16)

G27
(page 16)

G28
(page 17)

G29
(page 17)

G30
(page 18)

Flower, Heart, & Basket Blocks

F27
(page 18)

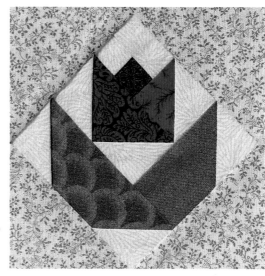

F28
(page 19)

F29
(page 19)

F30
(page 20)

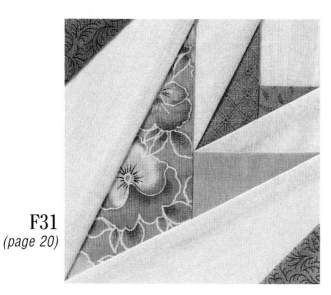

F31
(page 20)

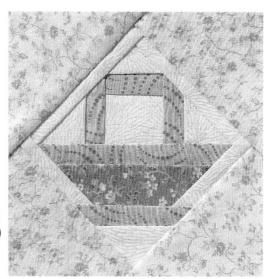

B12
(page 21)

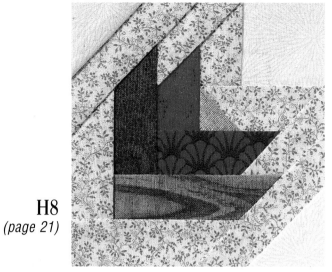

H8
(page 21)

H11
(page 22)

H12
(page 22)

Picture Blocks

P14
(page 26

P15
(page 26)

P16
(page 27)

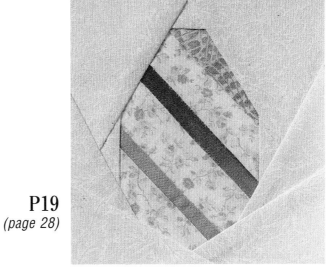

P17
(page 27)

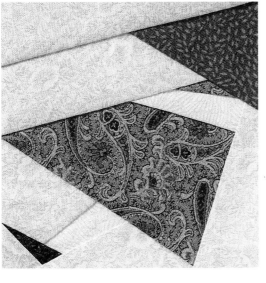

P18
(page 28)

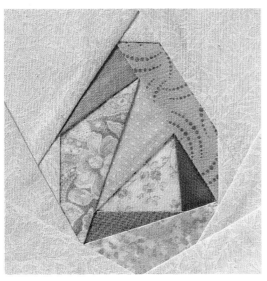

P19
(page 28)

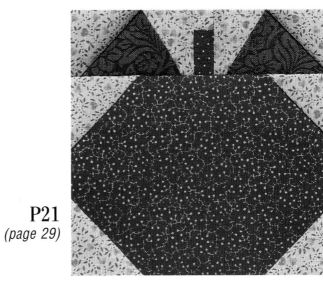

P20
(page 29)

P21
(page 29)

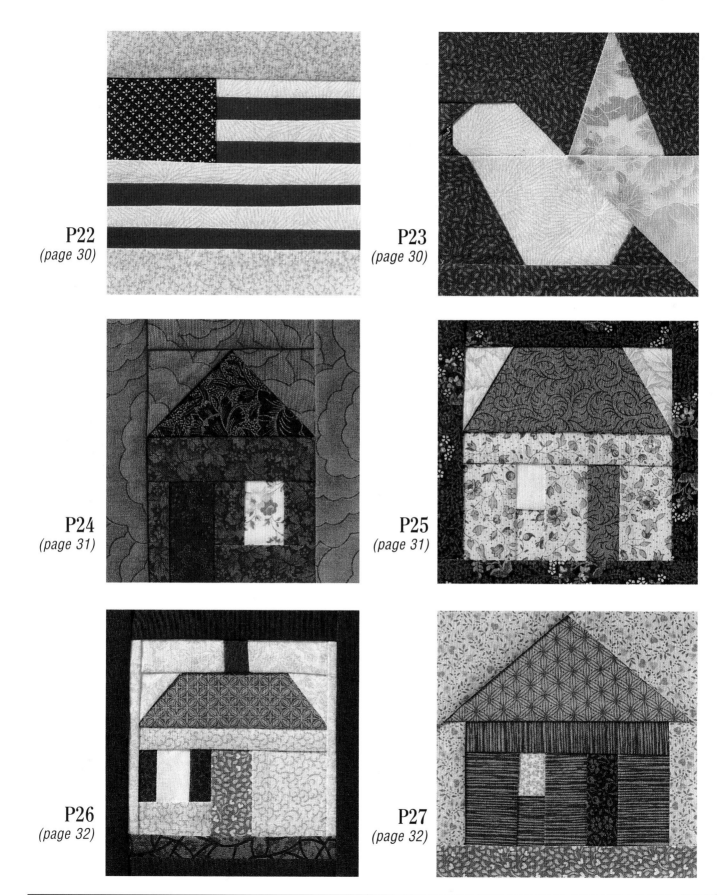

P22
(page 30)

P23
(page 30)

P24
(page 31)

P25
(page 31)

P26
(page 32)

P27
(page 32)

Block Designs

Christmas Blocks

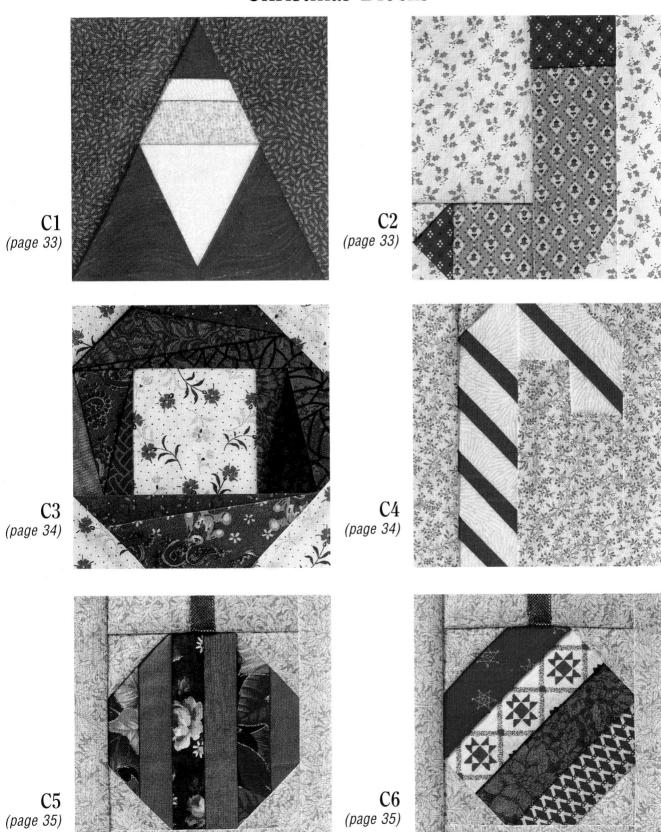

C1
(page 33)

C2
(page 33)

C3
(page 34)

C4
(page 34)

C5
(page 35)

C6
(page 35)

Christmas Blocks

C7
(page 36)

C8
(page 36)

C9
(page 37)

C10
(page 37)

C11
(page 38)

C12
(page 38)

Tree Blocks

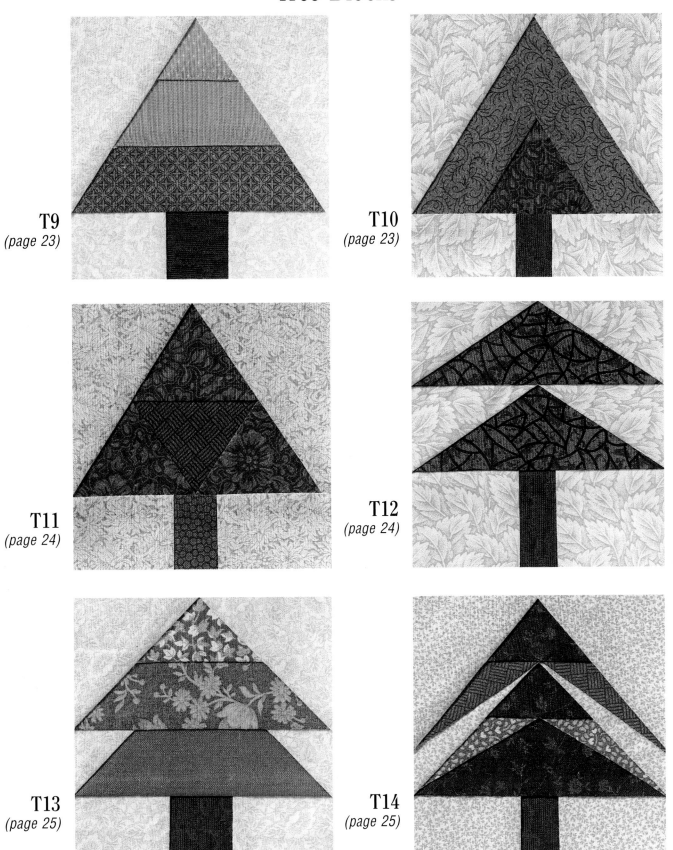

T9
(page 23)

T10
(page 23)

T11
(page 24)

T12
(page 24)

T13
(page 25)

T14
(page 25)

Gallery of Quilts

Calendar Quilt by Carol Doak, 1994, Windham, New Hampshire, 42" x 52". A variety of blocks celebrate the seasons and holidays, one for each month of the year. Carol used lots of scrap fabrics to create this multicolor quilt. The blocks would be fun to complete a month at a time.

School Days by Pamela Ludwig, 1994, Windham, New Hampshire, 24" x 36". This quilt celebrates "school days" and uses a variety of scrap fabrics. Little Apple and Letter blocks, used as corner squares in the border, are special details. This quilt, with an Americana flavor, would be ideal as a special wall decoration at the beginning of the school year or as a gift for a teacher.

Welcome Quilt *by Terry Maddox, 1994, Pelham, New Hampshire, 20" x 20". Terry used Letter blocks to spell out a warm welcome in the shape of a wreath. The quilt features a large Flower block in the center, and the message is punctuated with a small House block. This quick and easy little quilt makes a wonderful door decoration or wall quilt and gives you the chance to use a variety of fabrics from your scrap basket.*

Forest of Flowers by Helen Weinman, 1994, Centerville, Massachusetts, 48" x 60". Helen chose to shade both the flower fabrics and the green fabrics from light to dark to symbolize the changing of the seasons. She worked her beautiful machine quilting in a circular pattern through the Flower blocks and machine quilted through the tree-pattern papers to create the same tree in the lattice. The warm feelings of nature and color certainly shine through in this quilt.

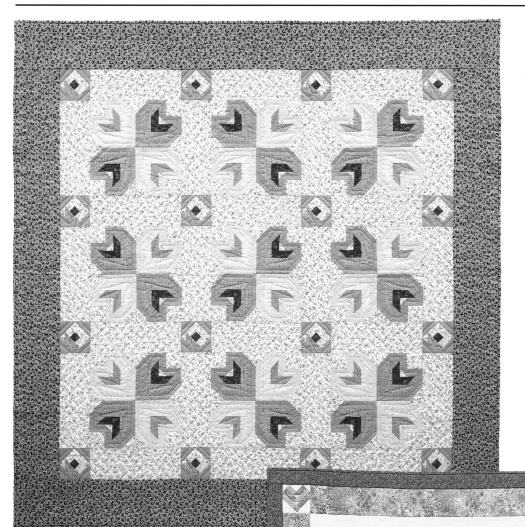

Hearts and Flowers by Carol Doak, 1994, Windham, New Hampshire, 64" x 64". Carol combined four Heart blocks worked in alternating color combinations to create the larger patchwork heart and flower designs. She set these larger designs in a lattice with smaller Flower block cornerstones. This design would make a nice wedding quilt or gift symbolizing love.

The Wedding Song by Marion Shelton, 1994, Redmond, Washington, 45" x 45". Marion combined the Nosegay and Heart blocks in this medallion-style quilt to convey a message of love. The darker floral portion of the background of the Nosegay blocks creates a subtle overall square on point. Soft pastel colors continue the theme and make this quilt a wonderful candidate for a wedding quilt or celebration of love.

Our World At Peace by Moira Clegg, 1994, Windham, New Hampshire, 42" x 42". Mo used the Bird block to symbolize the "Peace Dove," reversing the block to create this medallion-style arrangement. She changed the background fabric of the "Dove" block and used it in conjunction with a simple geometric block to create the overall square on point. Metallic gold thread in the feathered quilting design adds a bit of glitz. Using just two block designs makes this quilt quick and easy to make. You can feature pretty quilting designs in the large open areas.

Peace and Love by Mary Kay Sieve, 1994, Windham, New Hampshire, 36" x 45". These Letter blocks send a message of peace and love. Combined geometric blocks create radiating suns under which the "Peace Doves" rest. A large Flower block design continues the radiating quality. Heart and Flower blocks complement the theme in the last row of this symbolic quilt.

American As Apple Pie by Beth Meek, 1994, Windham, New Hampshire, 39" x 39". Tree, house, apple, and American flag designs combine with a geometric block to create this little Americana quilt with a homespun flavor. Smaller Apple blocks used as corner squares in the inner border add special detail. Beth added to the charm of this quilt by using small buttons for doorknobs on the House block doors. This quilt allows you to use up small pieces of fabric and decorate a wall at the same time.

Autumn Leaves by Carol Doak, 1994, Windham, New Hampshire, 41" x 41". This quilt uses just one simple Picture block to create a tessellating leaf design that offers the ultimate opportunity to use your scrap fabrics. This colorful quilt would bring the feeling of autumn to any wall at any time of the year.

With Love *by Carol Doak, 1994, Windham, New Hampshire, 42" x 30". This is an ideal baby quilt for a little girl. Carol used scrap fabrics for the patchwork Doll blocks. The alternating reverse block creates a delightful border around the center. Use the 3" blocks in the center to personalize this quilt for a special little someone.*

Tulip Time *by Sherry Reis, 1994, Worthington, Ohio, 60" x 60". Sherry combined two different geometric blocks with a Flower block and placed them in a Ninepatch setting to create larger patchwork blocks with a radiating quality. The larger block units are latticed with the same background fabric and set with patchwork cornerstones, creating a quilt of diamond stars and tulips that appear to float on the sky-like background. This quilt could decorate a wall or warm the body with the feeling of spring anytime.*

Sunrise Service *by Virginia L. Guaraldi, 1994, Londonderry, New Hampshire, 48" x 48". Virginia combined yellow scraps in the center of this medallion-style quilt to create the radiating sun. She used Flower blocks in the corners of the next design area and as corner squares in the last border to continue the radiating theme. This quilt could celebrate the beginning of Spring or the Easter holiday.*

Sampler Quilt by Carol Doak, 1994, Windham, New Hampshire, 27" x 33". This quilt is based on needlework samplers used by young girls in the past to learn their letters. Carol made the Bird blocks in shades of blue to symbolize the "blue bird of happiness," and she included a House block to symbolize the importance of home. This little quilt would make a wonderful baby quilt or wall decoration.

Smooth Sailing by Margaret Forand, 1994, Sutton Mills, New Hampshire, 42" x 42". Margaret combined two geometric block designs to create a radiating design around which a variety of patchwork ships sail. Blue fabrics continue the nautical theme and create a quiet setting for the colorful patchwork ships. You could easily include Letter blocks in the 3" lattice and border to personalize this quilt for a lover of the sea.

Santa Claus is Coming to Town by Carol Doak, 1994, Windham, New Hampshire, 22" x 22". Tree, House, and Santa blocks bring the feeling of Christmas to this wall quilt that is so quick and easy to make. If you are searching for a special Christmas gift for a special someone, "Santa Claus is Coming to Town" might just be your answer.

O Christmas Tree by Carol Doak, 1993, Windham, New Hampshire, 30" x 30". This little wall quilt features all the Christmas Ornament block designs placed in the setting of a tree. Use your red, green, and white scrap fabrics for the ornaments. This is another quilt that would make a great gift for someone special. Try personalizing the 3" border surrounding the tree with a family name.

Block and Quilt Design Possibilities

Eliminating and Adding Seam Lines

The block designs presented in this book represent only a fraction of the possible block variations. You can sew them as presented or create additional block design variations by simply eliminating one or more seams. You will not be arrested by the patchwork police if you don't piece all the sections of the blocks as they appear. You can eliminate any line if you can continue the piecing sequence without consequence. Eliminating seam lines not only creates a new design, but also simplifies the block so that it is quicker to piece. The illustration below shows how to make variations of the same block by eliminating seam lines.

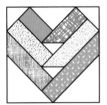 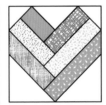

You can also *add* seam lines to create block-design variations if the piecing sequence continues across the added lines or if the added seam is the last seam. Additional seam lines can make a design more intricate or can actually simplify a block.

You can eliminate merging seams in the corner of a block by adding a seam across the corner. This is a helpful option if you plan to piece two or four blocks in rotation. Measure the same distance from the corner and connect the line. The merging corner seams are no more!

Seams that converge at a point create a seam-matching challenge and a bulky center.

Add a line across converging seams for easier piecing.

Block designs that benefit from an additional last seam line across the corner have a dotted line to indicate the added-seam variation.

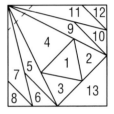

Exploring Value Options

Changing the value of the fabric in each area of the design can further increase the design possibilities. Value is the amount of lightness or darkness in colors; a black-and-white photograph shows only values. The same line drawing can offer a variety of design possibilities, depending upon the placement of the values. The following block looks very different when you change the values.

The same block with different value placement

You can experiment with value changes by coloring in sections of the block-front drawings with a lead pencil in light, medium, and dark shadings to discover other design options. Once you have decided on the values, use colored pencils to experiment with color in the design.

Making Fabric Choices

There are many fabric possibilities. You can use a group of coordinated fabrics to complete a project of the same block design or a combination of several block designs. You can select one fabric to set the theme or tone of your quilt and group fabrics that coordinate with this main fabric. Once you have established the theme for your keepsake quilt, consider how the choice of fabric can reinforce it. The following are just some of the possibilities:

- Turn a flower design into a Christmas quilt by using red and green Christmas fabrics or into a springtime quilt by using soft pastels.
- Red, white, and blue fabrics evoke a patriotic mood.
- Lavender and yellow fabrics bring Easter to mind.
- A flower or a basket in autumn colors creates a quilt that celebrates the season or Thanksgiving.
- Make a quilt for a new bride in the colors she has chosen for her bridesmaids' dresses.
- Make a quilt for a little girl using fabrics from her outgrown clothes as the dresses for the Doll blocks. Likewise, make a little boy's quilt with pieces of his outgrown clothing in the ships of the "Smooth Sailing" quilt on page 66.
- For a special friendship quilt, use a solid fabric that can be signed by friends or family members in one portion of a block.
- Family members coming home for Christmas could sign wreaths, stockings, or Christmas Ornament blocks. Friends and family could sign Heart or Flower blocks for a special wedding quilt. Students in a class could sign the Letter or Apple blocks to make a memorable quilt for a special teacher.
- Since the paper helps to stabilize the fabric and you use a short stitch, you can incorporate fabrics into your patchwork that you might not normally choose, such as lamés and silks. If using tracing paper to sew the blocks, specific elements printed on the fabric are easily centered inside the lines of the first piece for a special look.

Personalizing Your Quilts

The Letter blocks offer many opportunities to personalize your quilts with initials, family names, the name of the recipient of the quilt, or your name as the quiltmaker. Enlarging patchwork blocks to 6" and reducing the Letter blocks to 3" opens many avenues to follow. Many of the quilts in the Gallery of Quilts contain 3" borders where Letter blocks could easily be included. Try combining 3" squares with 3" Letter blocks and then surrounding them with 6" patchwork blocks, as in the "With Love" quilt on page 65.

Investigating Gift Ideas

Beyond making quilts, these paper-pieced designs offer the opportunity to make quick little gifts too. The Christmas Ornament blocks can be made into ornaments for the tree. Just make the block and pin the ends of a 6"-long piece of looped ribbon at the center top. Stitch a like-size fabric square to the block, right sides together, leaving a small section open on the bottom to turn the block right side out. Turn, press, and stitch the opening closed.

Fabric-backed, paper-pieced patchwork squares can also be made into pin cushions and sachets by filling the backed squares appropriately. Table runners and place mats are other small projects you can make using these paper-pieced blocks. The completed project can be backed with fabric and turned right side out. Center joined paper-pieced blocks on a fabric foundation the size of the desired project, and foundation-piece fabric strips until the foundation is completely covered.

You can make delightful little framed pictures by joining small patchwork designs and putting them under glass. I don't bother to remove the paper when I frame my paper-pieced patchwork. I select my frame size first and make the blocks and border the required size. To make a gift for a favorite teacher, place Letter blocks A, B, and C in one row with Heart and Apple blocks in the next row. Then add a border, mat, and frame. Even just one bordered block design makes a nice little gift.

Suggestion for paper-pieced blocks under glass

Quilt Layouts

To create original design keepsake quilts, make a quilt layout work sheet to try the block-front drawings in different positions and color schemes. On graph paper, draw a grid of 1" squares in a straight set or in a diagonal set, in the size you intend to make. Each square represents one block. Photocopy the grid layout for a ready supply of work sheets.

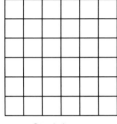 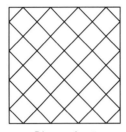

Straight set   Diagonal set

Select a group of blocks and cut out photocopies of the block-front drawings. Move the blocks around on the layout work sheet in different positions and rotations until you achieve a pleasing design. Consider using some plain fabric squares in between the patchwork blocks. Consider using borders and lattice strips to separate the blocks. Try different geometric blocks to see how they interact.

All the blocks do not have to be the same size. For example, 6" blocks and 3" blocks can easily be used in the same quilt. Borders that are 1" wide can be added to 4" blocks to create 6" blocks. Four 6" blocks can be combined to create a single 12" block that can be latticed for a full-size quilt. You can easily substitute different blocks for those in the Gallery of Quilts for a completely different design with the same quilt layout.

Project Size

To determine the size of a straight-set quilt layout, multiply the number of blocks vertically and horizontally by the size of the block chosen. For example, six blocks that are each 4" square make a 24" project without borders. Six 6" square blocks make a project that is 36" without borders.

For diagonal-set quilt layouts, multiply the size of the block by 1.4141 to arrive at the diagonal measurement of the block. For example, a 4" block set on the diagonal has a 5⅝" diagonal measurement. Multiply this number by the number of blocks in the quilt vertically and horizontally to determine the quilt length and width without borders.

Use half-square triangles (straight grain on the short side) for corner triangles by cutting a square once diagonally. Determine the finished size of the short edge of the triangle, add ⅞" to this figure, and cut a square that size.

Use quarter-square triangles (straight grain on the long side) for side triangles by cutting a square twice diagonally. Determine the finished size of the long side of the triangle, then add 1¼" and cut a square that size.

The following chart indicates the finished diagonal size of a variety of finished block sizes and the size squares to cut for the corner and side triangles.

Finished Block Size	Diagonal Size	Corner Triangles	Side Triangles
3"	4¼"	3"	5½"
4"	5⅝"	3¾"	6⅞"
5"	7⅛"	4½"	8⅜"
6"	8½"	5⅛"	9¾"
7"	9⅞"	5⅞"	11⅛"
8"	11⅜"	6⅝"	12⅝"

Keepsake Quilts

After I grouped the block designs for this book, I began to play with them to create a variety of quilt designs. I did not set out to make strictly "keepsake" quilts, but the designs seemed to lead me in that direction. It was easy to select a few block designs to fit the event or seasonal thought and play with the possibilities. So easy, in fact, that I finally made myself put the quilt designing on hold. I then had the dilemma that many quilters have—too many quilts to make and too little time! My friends came to the rescue and chose their favorite designs to make quilts for this book. They made wonderful quilts, adding their own special touches.

For each quilt, the Quilt Plan diagram indicates the block layout and borders. Measurements indicated in the quilt plans for borders, sashing, and squares are *cut* sizes and include ½"-wide seam allowances. Make photocopies of the quilt plan so you can experiment with different color schemes. Refer to the color photograph of the quilt or create your own color combination.

Each block design and color combination is assigned a letter. When a variation of a block design is used (as designated by [var.] after block number), the appropriate seam line(s) are eliminated or added to the design. See "Eliminating and Adding Seam Lines" on page 68. When the reverse of a design is used, the letter "r" follows the block number. See "Creating the Reverse of a Block" on page 6.

The Block Placement Guide indicates the placement of each block design and various color variations in the sample quilt.

Some quilts contain blocks reduced to 3". Others have blocks enlarged to 6". See "Enlarging and Reducing Block Designs" on page 5. The sizes of the blocks and borders used in the sample quilts are also provided; however, you can complete these projects in a variety of sizes by changing the sizes of the blocks and/or the borders.

Yardage

The yardage estimates for the sample quilts were calculated generously to allow for oversize cutting of pieces. When a small amount of fabric is used in one or two places in the quilt, a piece of fabric is given in inches. When small amounts of the same fabric are used several times in the quilt, a ⅛ yard minimum is given.

Cut larger pieces of fabric for borders, lattices, cornerstones, and bindings first; then use the remainder of the fabric to piece the blocks. Yardage requirements for the borders and backing are based on 41" of usable fabric after preshrinking and trimming away the selvages. If your fabric measures less than 41" you will need additional yardage. Yardage for bindings was calculated using 2"-wide strips cut across the width of the fabric (crosswise grain) unless otherwise noted.

A	C	E	D	C	A
C	F	G	G	F	C
D	G	A	B	G	E
E	G	B	A	G	D
C	F	G	G	F	C
A	C	D	E	C	A

Block Placement Guide

Calendar Quilt

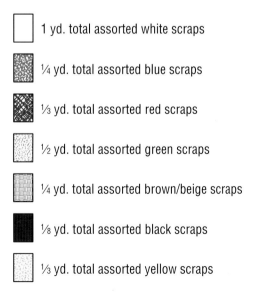

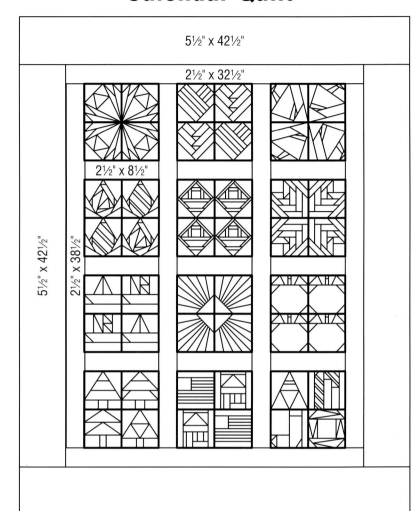

5½" x 42½"

2½" x 32½"

2½" x 8½"

5½" x 42½"

2½" x 38½"

Color photo on page 60
Finished Block Size: 4"
Finished Lattice: 2"
Finished Border: 5"
Finished Quilt Size: 42" x 52"
Measurements in Quilt Plan are cut sizes.

1 yd. total assorted white scraps

¼ yd. total assorted blue scraps

⅓ yd. total assorted red scraps

½ yd. total assorted green scraps

¼ yd. total assorted brown/beige scraps

⅛ yd. total assorted black scraps

⅓ yd. total assorted yellow scraps

¼ yd. total assorted pink scraps

⅛ yd. total assorted orange scraps

⅛ yd. total assorted purple scraps

¾ yd. dark blue for lattice

1½ yds. medium blue for
outer border and binding*

3⅓ yds. for backing

*Cut border and binding from
lengthwise grain of fabric.*

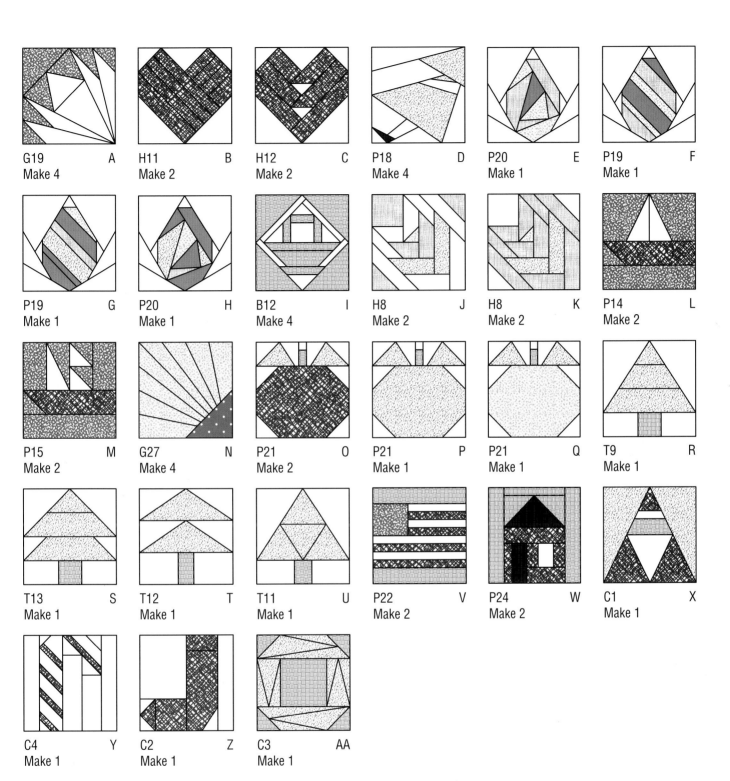

G19　　　A
Make 4

H11　　　B
Make 2

H12　　　C
Make 2

P18　　　D
Make 4

P20　　　E
Make 1

P19　　　F
Make 1

P19　　　G
Make 1

P20　　　H
Make 1

B12　　　I
Make 4

H8　　　J
Make 2

H8　　　K
Make 2

P14　　　L
Make 2

P15　　　M
Make 2

G27　　　N
Make 4

P21　　　O
Make 2

P21　　　P
Make 1

P21　　　Q
Make 1

T9　　　R
Make 1

T13　　　S
Make 1

T12　　　T
Make 1

T11　　　U
Make 1

P22　　　V
Make 2

P24　　　W
Make 2

C1　　　X
Make 1

C4　　　Y
Make 1

C2　　　Z
Make 1

C3　　　AA
Make 1

A	B	C	A
D			E
C	I		F
A	G	H	A

Color photo on page 61
Finished Block Sizes: 3" and 6"
Finished Border: 4"
Finished Quilt Size: 20" x 20"
Measurements in Quilt Plan are cut sizes.

Welcome Quilt

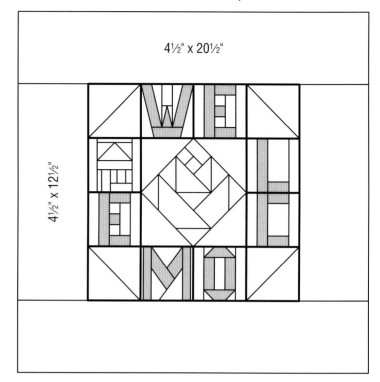

4½" x 20½"

4½" x 12½"

 ¼ yd. dark green

 ¼ yd. pink print for blocks and binding

 ¼ yd. total assorted light and medium scraps

 ⅓ yd. light floral print for block and border

⅔ yd. for backing

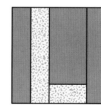

G30   A
Make 4
3" blocks

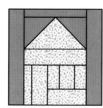

L23   B
Make 1
3" block

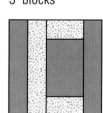

L5   C
Make 2
3" blocks

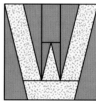

P24   D
Make 1
3" block

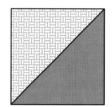

L12   E
Make 1
3" block

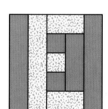

L3   F
Make 1
3" block

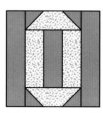

L13   G
Make 1
3" block

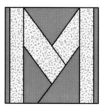

L15   H
Make 1
3" block

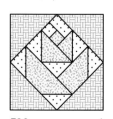

F28   I
Make 1
6" block

Sampler Quilt

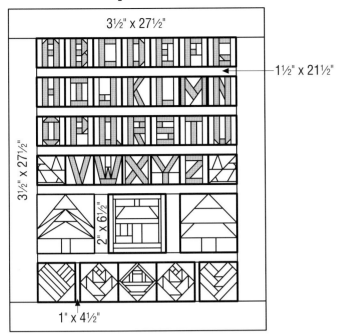

3½" x 27½"

1½" x 21½"

3½" x 27½"

2" x 6½"

1" x 4½"

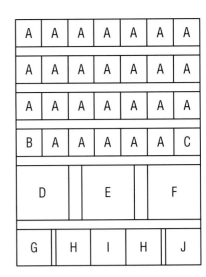

Color photo on page 66
Finished Block Sizes: 3", 4" and 6"
Finished Border: 3"
Finished Quilt Size: 27" x 33"
Measurements in Quilt Plan are cut sizes.

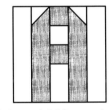

L1 through L26   A
Make 1 letter of the
alphabet; 3" blocks

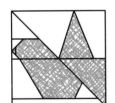

P23   B
Make 1
3" block

P23r   C
Make 1
3" block

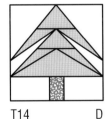

T14   D
Make 1
6" block

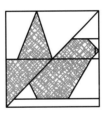

P26   E
Make 1
6" block

T13   F
Make 1
6" block

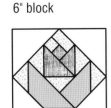

H11   G
Make 1
4" block

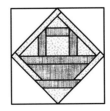

F28   H
Make 2
4" blocks

B12   I
Make 1
4" block

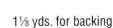

H12   J
Make 1
4" block

☐ ¾ yd. white

▦ ⅓ yd. total assorted scraps
   in medium shades

▦ ⅛ yd. total assorted blue scraps

▦ ⅛ yd. total assorted brown scraps
   (bird beak is brown)

▦ ⅛ yd. total assorted green scraps

▦ ⅛ yd. total assorted red scraps

☐ 1 yd. light blue for blocks, lattice,
   border, and binding

   1⅛ yds. for backing

Our World At Peace

D		A	A		C
	A	D	C	A	
A	D	A	A	C	A
A	B	A	A	E	A
	A	B	E	A	
B		A	A		E

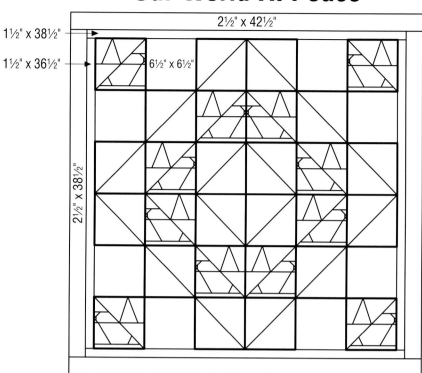

2½" x 42½"

1½" x 38½"

1½" x 36½"

6½" x 6½"

2½" x 38½"

Color photo on page 63
Finished Block Size: 6"
Finished Inner Border: 1"
Finished Outer Border: 2"
Finished Quilt Size: 42" x 42"
Measurements in Quilt Plan are cut sizes.

☐ ½ yd. white

▨ ¾ yd. pale blue for pieced blocks and plain blocks

⋰ 12 different light blue fabrics, each 6" x 6"

▨ ⅓ yd. assorted medium and dark blue scraps

▨ 8" x 8" solid yellow (bird beak is yellow)

¼ yd. gold print for inner border

1¼ yds. blue print for outer border and binding*

2½ yds. for backing

Cut border and binding from lengthwise grain of fabric.

G30 A
Make 16

P23 B
Make 3

P23 C
Make 3

P23r D
Make 3

P23r E
Make 3

Sunrise Service

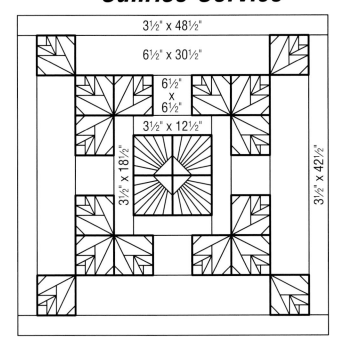

3½" x 48½"

6½" x 30½"

6½" x 6½"

3½" x 12½"

3½" x 18½"

3½" x 42½"

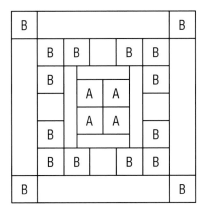

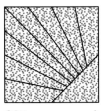

G27   A
Make 4

F31   B
Make 16

Color photo on page 65
Finished Block Size: 6"
Finished Inner Border: 3"
Finished Middle Border: 6"
Finished Outer Border: 3"
Finished Quilt Size: 48" x 48"
**Measurements in Quilt Plan
are cut sizes.**

□ 1 yd. white

■ ¼ yd. dark green

■ ¼ yd. medium purple

□ ⅛ yd. lavender

■ ⅛ yd. dark blue

▦ 1 yd. light blue for pieced blocks, plain blocks, and 6" middle border

▦ ½ yd. total assorted yellow/gold scraps

1½ yds. light green for inner and outer borders and binding*

3 yds. for backing

*Cut outer border and binding from lengthwise grain of fabric.

Tulip Time

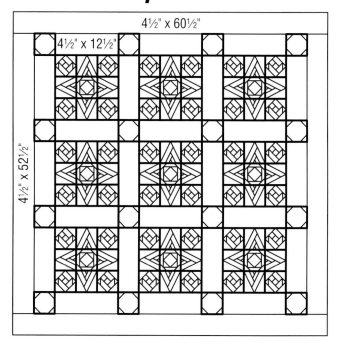

4½" x 60½"

4½" x 12½"

4½" x 52½"

Color photo on page 65
Finished Block Size: 4"
Finished Lattice: 4"
Finished Border: 4"
Finished Quilt Size: 60" x 60"
**Measurements in Quilt Plan
are cut sizes.**

☐ ½ yd. white

▨ ⅛ yd. medium gold

▨ ¾ yd. light gold

▨ ¾ yd. medium blue

☐ 2 yds. light blue for
blocks and lattice

▨ 2 yds. dark blue for blocks,
border, and binding*

4 yds. for backing

*Cut border and binding from
lengthwise grain of fabric.

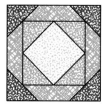

G29   A
Make 9

G28   B
Make 36

F27   C
Make 18

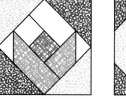

F27   D
Make 18

G29 (var.)   E
Make 16

Hearts and Flowers

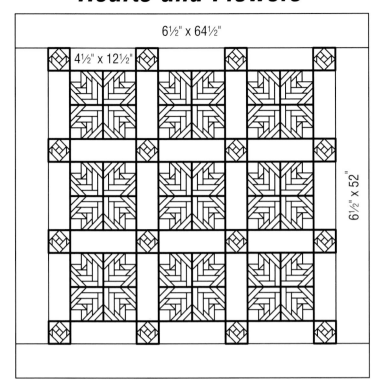

6½" x 64½"

4½" x 12½"

6½" x 52"

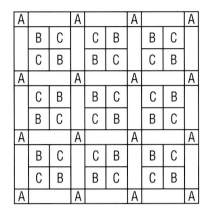

Color photo on page 62
Finished Block Sizes: 4" and 6"
Finished Lattice: 4" x 12"
Finished Border: 6"
Finished Quilt Size: 64" x 64"
Measurements in Quilt Plan are cut sizes.

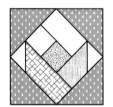

F27   A
Make 16
4" blocks

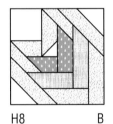

H8   B
Make 18
6" blocks

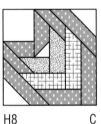

H8   C
Make 18
6" blocks

2 yds. white for blocks and lattice

1 yd. light pink

1½ yds. medium pink

⅓ yd. dark pink

½ yd. medium green

⅓ yd. light green

2 yds. dark green for border and binding*

4 yds. for backing

*Cut outer border and binding from lengthwise grain of fabric.

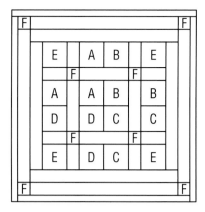

Color photo on page 62
Finished Block Sizes: 3" and 6"
Finished Lattice: 3"
Finished Borders: 3" and 1½"
Finished Quilt Size: 45" x 45"
**Measurements in Quilt Plan
are cut sizes.**

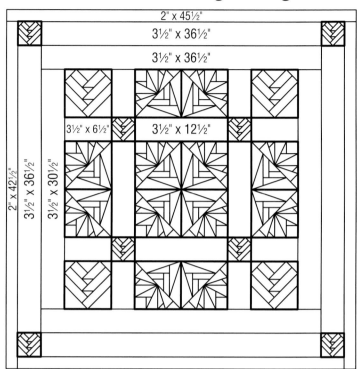

2" x 45½"

3½" x 36½"

3½" x 36½"

3½" x 6½"   3½" x 12½"

2" x 42½"

3½" x 36½"

3½" x 30½"

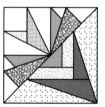

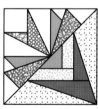

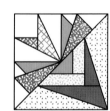

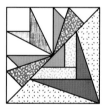

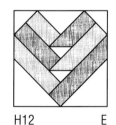

☐ ½ yd. white

1 yd. floral print for blocks
and second border

1⅓ yds. darkest green for
blocks, outer border, and binding*

⅓ yd. medium green

¼ yd. lighter green

⅛ yd. lightest green

9" x 4" medium blue scrap

2" x 8" light blue scrap

9" x 4" medium purple scrap

2" x 8" light purple scrap

9" x 4" medium yellow scrap

2" x 8" light yellow scrap

¼ yd. medium pink

¼ yd. light pink

1⅛ yds. pale pink for lattice
and inner border

2¾ yds. for backing

*Cut outer border and binding
from lengthwise grain of fabric.

F29   A
Make 3
6" blocks

F29   B
Make 3
6" blocks

F29   C
Make 3
6" blocks

F29   D
Make 3
6" blocks

H12   E
Make 4
6" blocks

H12   F
Make 8
3" blocks

With Love

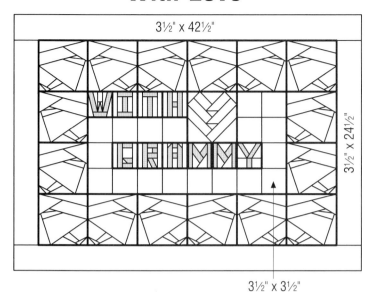

3½" x 42½"

3½" x 24½"

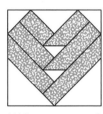

3½" x 3½"

A	B	A	B	A	B
B	D E F G		C		A
A	H I J K K L				B
B	A	B	A	B	A

Color photo on page 65
Finished Block Sizes: 3" and 6"
Finished Border: 3"
Finished Quilt Size: 42" x 30"
Measurements in Quilt Plan are cut sizes.

1 yd. light print

16 squares, each 8" x 8", of assorted medium fabrics. One hat and one dress can be cut from each square.

⅛ yd. black

⅝ yd. white for pieced blocks and plain blocks

¼ yd. assorted medium fabrics

1⅜ yds. blue print for border and binding*

1⅜ yds. for backing

* Cut border and binding from lengthwise grain of fabric.

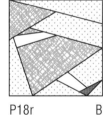

P18   A
Make 8
6" blocks

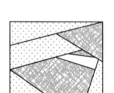

P18r   B
Make 8
6" blocks

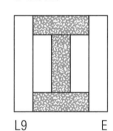

H12   C
Make 1
6" block

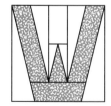

L23   D
Make 1
3" block

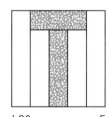

L9   E
Make 1
3" block

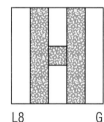

L20   F
Make 1
3" block

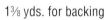
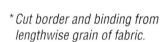

L8   G
Make 1
3" block

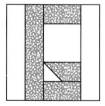

L7   H
Make 1
3" block

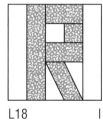

L18   I
Make 1
3" block

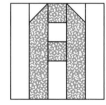

L1   J
Make 1
3" block

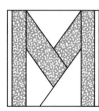

L13   K
Make 2
3" blocks

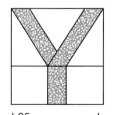

L25   L
Make 1
3" block

H				H
F	B	C	B	F
A	G	I	G	A
D	J	E	J	D
A	G	I	G	A
F	B	C	B	F
H				H

Color photo on page 64
Finished Block Sizes: 3" and 6"
Finished Inner Border: 3"
Finished Outer Border: 1½"
Finished Quilt Size: 39" x 39"
Measurements in Quilt Plan are cut sizes.

American as Apple Pie

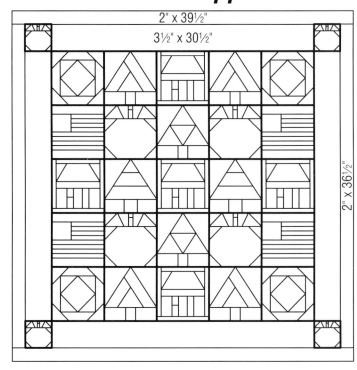

2" x 39½"
3½" x 30½"
2" x 36½"

 ¾ yd. beige

¹⁄₈ yd. dark blue

¹⁄₈ yd. solid white

¹⁄₈ yd. red #1

¼ yd. red #2

¹⁄₈ yd. red #3

½ yd. light blue

¼ yd. dark green

¼ yd. medium green

¼ yd. light green

¹⁄₈ yd. dark brown

¹⁄₈ yd. black

¹⁄₈ yd. med. brown #1

¹⁄₈ yd. med. brown #3

¾ yd. med. brown #2 for blocks, outer border, and binding

¹⁄₃ yd. navy blue

½ yd. lt. blue for inner border

1¼ yds. for backing

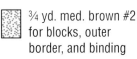

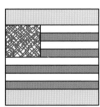
P22   A
Make 4
6" blocks

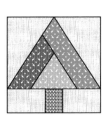
T10   B
Make 4
6" blocks

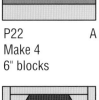
P25   C
Make 2
6" blocks

P25   D
Make 2
6" blocks

P25   E
Make 1
6" block

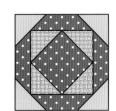
G29   F
Make 4
6" blocks

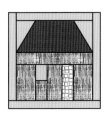
P21   G
Make 4
6" blocks

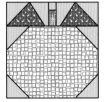
P21   H
Make 4
3" blocks

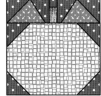
T11   I
Make 2
6" blocks

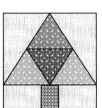
T9   J
Make 2
6" blocks

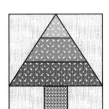

Smooth Sailing

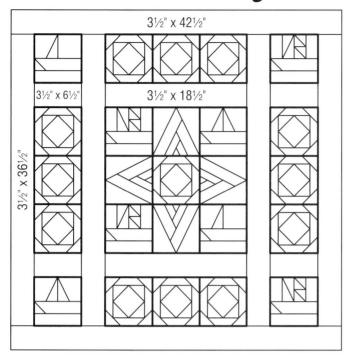

3½" x 42½"

3½" x 6½"

3½" x 18½"

3½" x 36½"

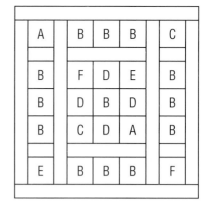

A	B	B	B	C
B	F	D	E	B
B	D	B	D	B
B	C	D	A	B
E	B	B	B	F

Color photo on page 66
Finished Block Size: 6"
Finished Lattice: 3"
Finished Border: 3"
Finished Quilt Size: 42" x 42"
Measurements in Quilt Plan are cut sizes.

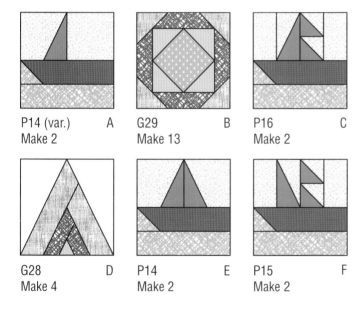

P14 (var.) A
Make 2

G29 B
Make 13

P16 C
Make 2

G28 D
Make 4

P14 E
Make 2

P15 F
Make 2

¼ yd. light blue sky fabric

¼ yd. light green print

⅛ yd. solid red

⅛ yd. total assorted bright solid scraps

½ yd. dark blue for blocks and binding

¼ yd. light blue

⅛ yd. medium dark blue

⅓ yd. medium blue

1¼ yds. white/blue print for blocks, lattice, and border*

2½ yds. backing

*Cut border and lattice from lengthwise grain of fabric.

Peace and Love

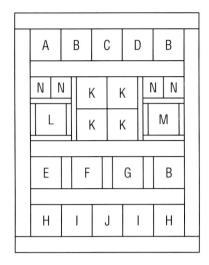

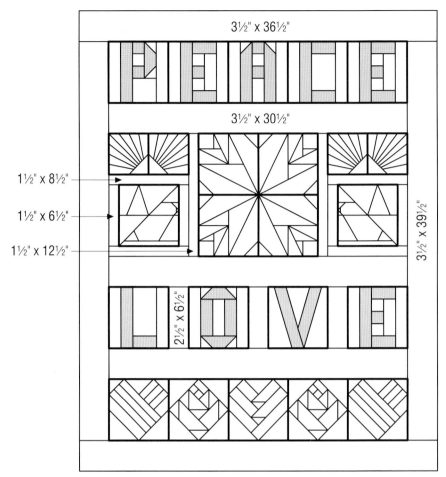

3½" x 36½"

3½" x 30½"

1½" x 8½"

1½" x 6½"

1½" x 12½"

2½" x 6½"

3½" x 39½"

Color photo on page 63
Finished Block Sizes: 4" and 6"
Finished Outer Border: 3"
Finished Quilt Size: 36" x 45"
**Measurements in Quilt Plan
are cut sizes.**

2 yds. white for blocks,
lattice and borders

⅓ yd. light green

½ yd. total assorted
medium pink scraps

¼ yd. medium blue

2" x 9" green

⅛ yd. print for the bird

1½" x 14" dark gray

¼ yd. total assorted
yellow scraps (bird
beak is yellow)

⅓ yd. for binding

1½ yds. for backing

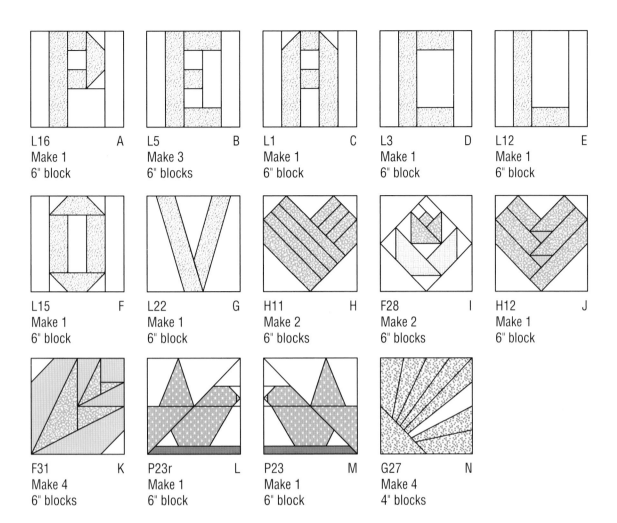

L16   A
Make 1
6" block

L5   B
Make 3
6" blocks

L1   C
Make 1
6" block

L3   D
Make 1
6" block

L12   E
Make 1
6" block

L15   F
Make 1
6" block

L22   G
Make 1
6" block

H11   H
Make 2
6" blocks

F28   I
Make 2
6" blocks

H12   J
Make 1
6" block

F31   K
Make 4
6" blocks

P23r   L
Make 1
6" block

P23   M
Make 1
6" block

G27   N
Make 4
4" blocks

Forest of Flowers

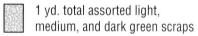
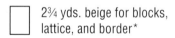
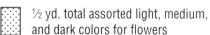

4½" x 48½"

4½" x 8½"

4½" x 52"

Color photo on page 61
Finished Block Size: 4"
Finished Lattice: 4"
Finished Border: 4"
Finished Quilt Size: 48" x 60"
**Measurements in Quilt Plan
are cut sizes.**

2¾ yds. beige for blocks,
lattice, and border*

1 yd. total assorted light,
medium, and dark green scraps

½ yd. total assorted light, medium,
and dark colors for flowers

⅛ yd. dark brown

½ yd. for binding. (Helen chose to piece
leftover strips of flower fabrics to create
a pieced binding that shades from light
to dark. If you want to take this
approach, you need to increase your
flower fabrics to 1 yd. and you need
approximately 226" of 2" wide binding.)

3¾ yds. for backing

Cut border from lengthwise grain of fabric.

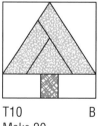
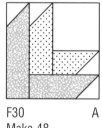

F30   A   T10   B
Make 48   Make 20

Helen used the same flower and leaf fabrics for two blocks in
each four-block unit and placed these blocks diagonally. Both
the flower and leaf fabrics begin in
light shades at the top of the quilt
and gradually become darker toward the bottom. The same gradual
light-to-dark transition takes place
in the Tree blocks as well.

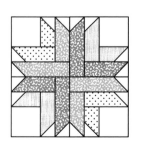

School Days

3½" x 18½"

3½" x 30½"

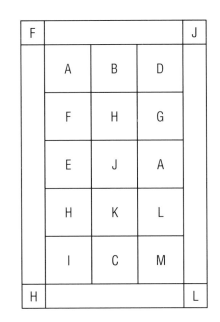

F				J
	A	B	D	
	F	H	G	
	E	J	A	
	H	K	L	
	I	C	M	
H				L

□ ¾ yd. assorted light scraps

▨ 3" x 6" dark brown

▨ ¼ yd. assorted green scraps

▨ ½ yd. assorted red scraps

▨ ¼ yd. assorted blue scraps

½ yd. navy blue border and binding fabric

¾ yd. for backing

Color photo on page 60
Finished Block Sizes: 3" and 6"
Finished Border: 3"
Finished Quilt Size: 24" x 36"
Measurements in Quilt Plan are cut sizes.

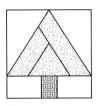

T10   A
Make 2
6" blocks

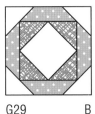

G29   B
Make 1
6" block

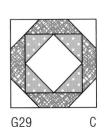

G29   C
Make 1
6" block

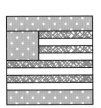

P22   D
Make 1
6" block

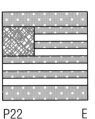

P22   E
Make 1
6" block

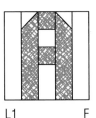

L1   F
Make 1 each
6" and 3" block

P25   G
Make 1
6" block

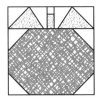

P21   H
Make one 3"
and two 6" blocks

P25   I
Make 1
6" block

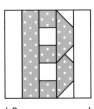

L2   J
Make 1 each
6" and 3" block

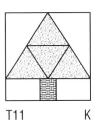

T11   K
Make 1
6" block

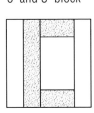

L3   L
Make 1 each
6" and 3" block

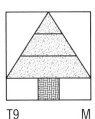

T9   M
Make 1
6" Block

A	B	A	B	A	B	A	B
B	A	B	A	B	A	B	A
A	B	A	B	A	B	A	B
B	A	B	A	B	A	B	A
A	B	A	B	A	B	A	B
B	A	B	A	B	A	B	A
A	B	A	B	A	B	A	B
B	A	B	A	B	A	B	A

Autumn Leaves

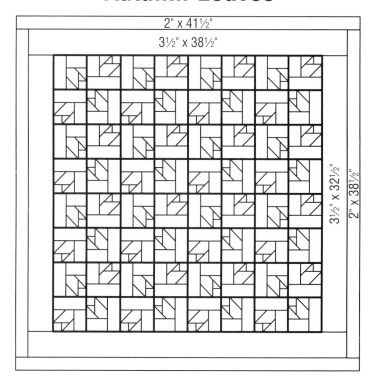

2" x 41½"

3½" x 38½"

3½" x 32½"

2" x 38½"

Color photo on page 64
Finished Block Size: 4"
Finished Inner Border: 3"
Finished Outer Border: 1½"
Finished Quilt Size: 41" x 41"
Measurements in Quilt Plan are cut sizes.

1 yd. total assorted red/orange/yellow scraps

1 yd. total assorted green scraps

¾ yd. white for blocks and inner border

1¼ yds. red for outer border and binding*

1⅓ yds. for backing**

* Cut border and binding from the lengthwise grain of fabric.

** The 41" finished width is cutting this pretty close. I was able to back this quilt with one width. If your backing fabric shrinks a good deal, you may need to join two widths.

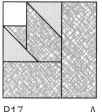

P17   A
Make 32

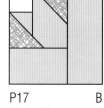

P17   B
Make 32

Tip: Pin all the paper patterns, blank side up, in the correct position on a sheet and mark the alternating red and green scrap blocks. As you cut the red and green fabrics for block A in the upper left corner, cut the remainder of the needed green fabrics to complete the two green leaves that adjoin it. Pin the green fabrics to the correct blocks so they are ready-cut when you piece those three adjoining blocks. Continue in this manner and cut the needed fabrics for each leaf color.

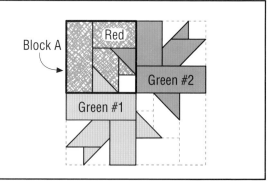

Block A — Red — Green #2 — Green #1

Santa Claus is Coming to Town

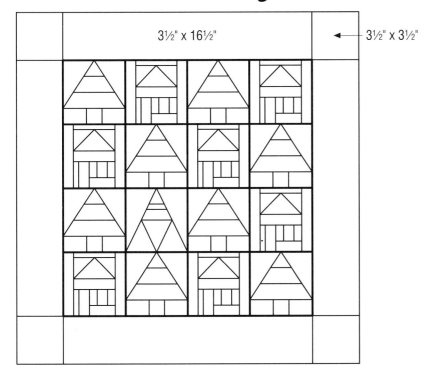

3½" x 16½"

← 3½" x 3½"

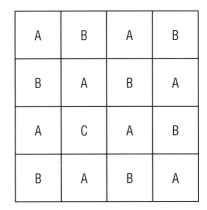

A	B	A	B
B	A	B	A
A	C	A	B
B	A	B	A

Color photo on page 67
Finished Block Size: 4"
Finished Border: 3"
Finished Quilt Size: 22" x 22"
Measurements in Quilt Plan are cut sizes.

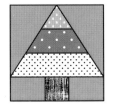

T9   A
Make 8

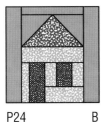

P24   B
Make 7

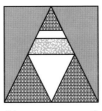

C1   C
Make 1

⅔ yd. black for blocks and binding

⅛ yd. black and white roof

¼ yd. total assorted beige scraps

⅛ yd. total assorted multicolor scraps

3" x 6" red

3" x 4" white

⅛ yd. green #1

⅛ yd. green #2

⅛ yd. green #3

⅛ yd. brown

¼ yd. red for border

⅛ yd. black for cornerstones

¾ yd. backing fabric

O Christmas Tree

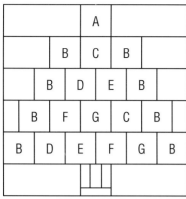

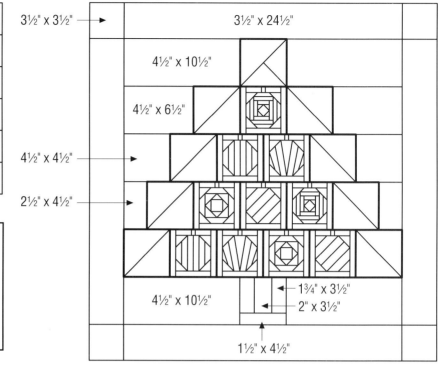

3½" x 3½"

3½" x 24½"

4½" x 10½"

4½" x 6½"

4½" x 4½"

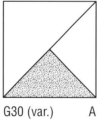

2½" x 4½"

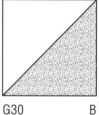

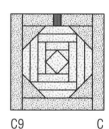

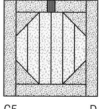

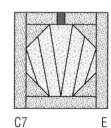

1¾" x 3½"

2" x 3½"

4½" x 10½"

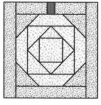

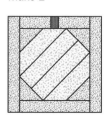

1½" x 4½"

Color photo on page 67
Finished Block Size: 4"
Finished Border: 3"
Finished Quilt Size: 30" x 30"
Measurements in Quilt Plan are cut sizes.

□ ½ yd. lightest green for blocks and background

▓ ½ yd. darkest green

▒ ½ yd. total assorted red, green, and white scraps

█ 1" x 12" metallic gold fabric

3" x 4" brown for trunk

½ yd. green for border and binding

⅛ yd. red for cornerstones

G30 (var.) A
Make 1*

G30 B
Make 8

C9 C
Make 2

C5 D
Make 2

C7 E
Make 2

C8 F
Make 2

C6 G
Make 2

To make this block variation, draw a diagonal line from corner to center and paper-piece units as 1a, 1b, and 2.

Quilt Finishing

Joining Blocks

Arrange the blocks and fabric units as shown in the block placement guide for the quilt you are making. To join blocks, place them right sides together, matching the appropriate seam lines. Place pins through the lines of both blocks and stitch along the marked line of the block. I machine baste important matching points before sewing the seam to check for a good match. Once the seam is machine basted, open it for a quick check to make sure the seams align correctly. If they do, proceed to sew the seam. If they don't quite match, remove the machine basting by clipping the thread from the bobbin side and pulling it out. Then try again. Basting at these crucial matching points also secures the area so it won't shift while sewing. Machine basting takes just a few minutes and eliminates a lot of frustration.

■ **Tip:** Place a block with points at the outside edge facing up as you sew the seam. This way you will be sure you sew across the point and not through it. If both blocks have points, have faith!

Press the seams in opposite directions from row to row. Pressing in this manner locks the seams into a good match. Sew the rows together, making sure to match the seams between each block.

■ **Tip:** If the outside edges of your blocks are mostly one color, change the thread to match.

Adding Borders

The quilts in this book are completed with straight-cut corners and corner squares.

Straight-Cut Corners

1. Measure the length of the quilt top at the center, from raw edge to raw edge, and cut two border strips to match that measurement. Mark the centers of the border strips and the sides of the quilt top; join the borders to the sides, matching center marks and edges and easing as necessary. Press the seams toward the borders.

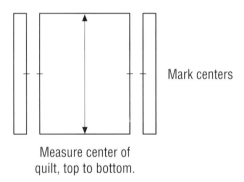

Mark centers

Measure center of
quilt, top to bottom.

2. Measure the width of the quilt top through the center, from raw edge to raw edge, including the border pieces just added; cut two border strips to match that measurement. Mark the centers of the border strips and the top and bottom of the quilt top; join the border strips to the top and bottom edges, matching centers and ends and easing as necessary. Press the seams toward the borders.

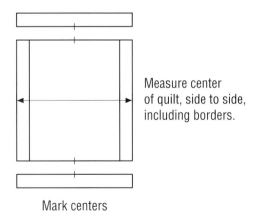

Measure center
of quilt, side to side,
including borders.

Mark centers

Borders with Corner Squares

1. Measure for all four border strips before adding side borders as described for borders with straight-cut corners. Sew the border strips to opposite sides of the quilt top first; press the seams toward the borders.

2. Attach the corner squares to the top and bottom strips and press the seams toward the border strips. Sew these strips to the top and bottom edges of the quilt top, matching the corner square seams with the side border seams.

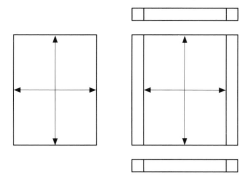

Removing the Paper and Pressing the Blocks

Remove the paper only after the completed blocks have been joined to other blocks or borders. A slight tug against the seam loosens the paper from the stitching. Use a small pair of tweezers to lift the paper along the stitching line and remove pieces of paper left behind. Don't concern yourself with tiny pieces of paper. They will only add warmth to the quilt!

Once the paper has been removed, press the blocks gently with a dry iron in an up-and-down motion. Dragging a steam iron across the blocks distorts them.

Basting the Quilt

Once the paper is removed, you are ready to sandwich and baste the top. The sandwich consists of the backing, the batting, and the quilt top. There are many types of quilt batting available. Use a thin, low-loft batting for small wall quilts—they don't need to keep the wall warm. The low-loft batting also helps you to take smaller stitches when quilting the smaller-scale designs. Cut the backing and the batting 2" to 3" larger than the quilt top all around.

1. Spread the backing, wrong side up, on a clean surface. Use masking tape or large binder clamps to anchor the backing to the table, being careful not to stretch it out of shape.

2. Spread and smooth the quilt batting over the backing. Make sure it covers the entire backing.

3. Place the quilt top on the batting, right side up, smoothing out any wrinkles. Make sure the edges of the quilt top are parallel to the edges of the backing.

4. Beginning in the middle and working to the outside edges, make diagonal, vertical, and horizontal rows of basting stitches in a grid. An alternative method is pin-basting with size 2, rustproof safety pins.

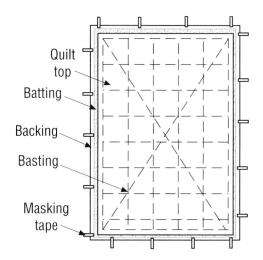

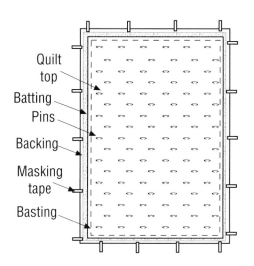

5. To contain any exposed batting while quilting, bring the edge of the backing around to the front of the quilt top and baste in place.

Quilting the Quilt

These quilts can be hand quilted, machine quilted, or a combination of both. If you prefer hand quilting, keep in mind that piecing tiny blocks with this method does not leave large areas of single-layer fabric available for hand quilting, so plan accordingly. You might want to alternate solid squares and/or add plain fabric borders to showcase your hand quilting. On the other hand, small projects composed of miniature blocks can be machine quilted easily. Remember too, that if you use a polyester batting requiring quilting at 3" to 4" intervals, your paper-pieced project of 4" block designs will not require much quilting.

One of my friends, Helen Weinman, used the paper-pieced pattern designs as guides for machine quilting. Helen simply made photocopies of the Tree block she used in her "Forest of Flowers" quilt on page 61, pinned the paper patterns on the lattice, and machine quilted the shape of the tree through the paper. Once the machine quilting was complete, she tore the paper away from the stitching.

Begin quilting the project in the middle and work toward the outside in a consistent fashion. It is similar to wallpapering, where you smooth the bubbles out toward the outside edges of the panel.

Adding a Sleeve

The preferred method for hanging a wall quilt is to slip a rod through a sleeve sewn on the back of the quilt. You can use the same fabric as the backing so it will blend in, or simply use a piece of muslin.

1. Cut a strip of fabric as long as the side of the quilt; double the size of the desired width and add ½" for seam allowances. Hem both ends of the strip.

2. Fold the strip, wrong sides together, and pin the raw edges at the top of the quilt before you attach the binding. Machine baste in place ⅛" from the edge. Add the binding to the quilt as described at right.

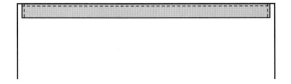

3. Blindstitch the folded edge of the sleeve to the back of the quilt.

Binding the Edges

Once you complete the quilting, it is time to bind the quilt. Prepare the quilt by removing the basting stitches and trimming the batting and backing even with the edge of the quilt top. Using a walking foot or an even-feed foot on your sewing machine, if available, sew a basting stitch around the perimeter of the quilt, approximately ⅛" from the edge. The even-feed foot aids in sewing all three layers smoothly. If adding a sleeve to hang your quilt project, baste it in place now. See "Adding a Sleeve" at left. Because the edges of wall quilts do not receive stress from handling, I prefer to use straight-grain binding on them. I use fabric strips cut on the bias when binding bed quilts because bias strips are stronger.

To make straight-grain binding:

1. Cut 2"-wide strips across the width of the fabric (crosswise grain), and sew the ends together at a 45° angle to make a strip long enough to go around the outside edges of the quilt, plus about 10". Trim the excess fabric at the seams and press them open.

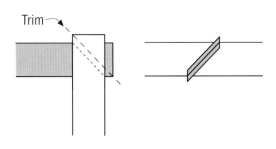
Trim

2. Fold the binding strip in half lengthwise, wrong sides together, and press.

3. Place the binding on the front of the quilt, lining up the raw edges of the binding with the raw edges of the quilt. Use a walking foot to sew the binding to the quilt with a ¼"-wide seam; leave the first few

inches of the binding loose so that you can join the beginning and ending of the binding strip later.

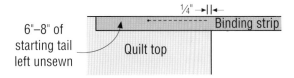

4. Stop stitching ¼" from the corner of the quilt and backstitch. Turn the quilt to sew the next edge. Fold the binding up and away from the quilt and then down, even with the next side. The straight fold should be even with the top edge of the quilt. Stitch from the edge to the next corner, stopping ¼" from the corner. Repeat for the remaining corners.

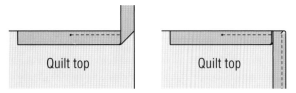

5. As you approach the beginning of the binding, stop; overlap the binding ½" from the start of the binding strip and trim the excess. Open the folds of the two strips and sew the ends together with a ¼"-wide seam allowance. Press the seam allowance open. Return the joined strip to the edge and finish the seam.

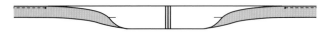

6. Fold the binding to the back over the raw edges of the quilt. The folded edge of the binding should cover the machine-stitching line. Blindstitch the binding in place. As you fold the binding to the back of the quilt, mitered corners form. Stitch them in place as shown.

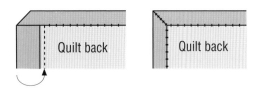

Signing Your Work

Your keepsake quilt is an expression of you. Be sure to make a label for the back of the quilt containing information such as your name, the date the quilt was completed, the name of the quilt, your town, the recipient of a gift quilt, and any other information you would like to add. The label can be as simple as writing on a piece of fabric or as elaborate as decorative stitching. One of the paper-pieced blocks can serve as your label if there is a large enough plain area for the writing or stitching you want to do.

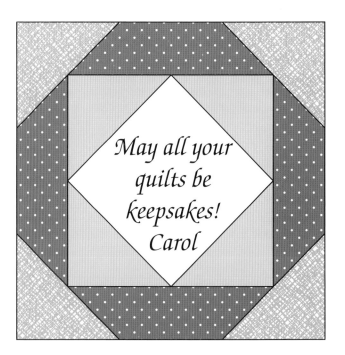

About the Author

Carol Doak is an award-winning quiltmaker, author, and teacher. She began teaching others how to make quilts in 1980, in Worthington, Ohio. Carol's teaching has taken her to many cities in the United States and recently to Australia to share her quiltmaking "Tricks of the Trade." She writes a regular column of the same title for *Quick and Easy Quilting* magazine. Her lighthearted approach and ability to teach have earned her high marks and positive comments from workshop participants.

Carol's quilts have been presented in several books, such as *Great American Quilts 1990* and *The Quilt Encyclopedia*. She has been featured in several national quilt magazines and her quilts have appeared on the covers of *Quilter's Newsletter Magazine, Quilt World, Quilting Today,* and *McCall's Quilting.*

Carol's first book, *Quiltmaker's Guide: Basics & Beyond,* was published in 1992. Her second book, *Country Medallion Sampler,* published in 1993, combines a medallion-style quilt with a country theme. Carol's third book, *Easy Machine Paper Piecing,* set into motion a passion for designing and creating patchwork quilts that could be made using this quick and easy method. *Easy Machine Paper Piecing* was so well received by quiltmakers that it went to a fourth printing in only six months! Carol used some of her paper-pieced block designs and quick foundation-piecing methods to create the wearables featured in her fourth book, *Easy Reversible Vests.*

Carol lives with her family in Windham, New Hampshire, where the snow-filled winter months provide a pretty picture to contemplate as she keeps cozy under quilts in progress.

Publications and Products

Many titles are available at your local quilt shop.
For more information, write for a free color catalo
to That Patchwork Place, Inc., PO Box 118, Both
WA 98041-0118 USA.

☎ U.S. and Canada, call **1-800-426-3126** for the
name and location of the quilt shop nearest you.
Int'l: 1-206-483-3313   Fax: 1-206-486-7596
E-mail: info@patchwork.com
Web: www.patchwork.com